Will the Soviet Union
Survive Until 1984?

ABOUT THE AUTHOR

Andrei Amalrik, historian, journalist and
playwright, was born in Russia in 1938. He was
expelled from Moscow University in 1963 for
political reasons, and in 1965 was sentenced to
two and a half years' exile for 'parasitism'. He was
allowed to return to Moscow at the end of 1966
but in 1970 he was arrested again and after spending
three and a half years in prison and prison camp was
once more sentenced to two years of exile in Siberia.

Andrei Amalrik left the Soviet Union in 1976 and lived
in exile in France. He was killed in an automobile
accident in Spain in November 1980.

Will the Soviet Union Survive Until 1984?

Andrei Amalrik

Edited by Hilary Sternberg

Revised and Expanded Edition

HARPER COLOPHON BOOKS
Harper & Row, Publishers
New York, Cambridge, Hagerstown, Philadelphia, San Francisco
London, Mexico City, São Paulo, Sydney

The Acknowledgements appearing on pages 223 and 224 constitute an extension of this copyright page.

Will the Soviet Union Survive Until 1984? was first published in the Russian language by the Alexander Herzen Foundation, Amsterdam, The Netherlands.

First HARPER COLOPHON edition published 1981.

ISBN: 0-06-090732-0

81 82 83 84 85 10 9 8 7 6 5 4 3 2 1

Contents

Preface to the Second English Edition

It was with great pleasure that I learned that a new edition of my book was to be published in England. Several years had passed since the first edition appeared; while I had languished in prison the world had not stood still, and I had decided that the book needed to be carefully re-read and various corrections and additions made. However, my friend Professor van het Reve dissuaded me from making any alterations on the grounds that this slim volume had become a 'historical document' of a kind and as such needed no emendation: it would be just as unthinkable as if somebody – be it Stalin himself – had set about correcting the 'genial utterances of comrade Stalin' at a later date.

True, Stalin did correct himself according to changing circumstances, as anyone who compared successive editions of his articles may become convinced for himself. Perhaps I have a better feeling for circumstances than comrade Stalin, perhaps I have more confidence in myself than he did, but, having re-read my essay, I see that it can be reprinted without any changes: I still agree with almost everything I wrote in 1969, and it seems to me that the last few years have borne out my analysis.

Certain things, however, must be said.

Firstly, I would not want my essay to be interpreted as any kind of *Schadenfreude* or death-wish with respect to the USSR. The book's aim is to indicate – perhaps in rather dramatic form – the dangers which threaten the Soviet Union. It is my wish that the Soviet Union, by way of democratic reorganization and a far-sighted foreign policy, should succeed in avoiding breakdown into a situation of anarchy and war.

Secondly, one should not draw from the book the conclusion, which some Party apparatchiks in the USSR have ascribed to me, that the entire Soviet people is of an 'anti-Soviet' disposition. If a certain section of the people had not actively supported the regime and a significant proportion had not passively accepted it, it would not have survived for sixty years. However, this support is being more and more eroded.

Thirdly, the validity of my remark that Soviet society is an immobile society has been questioned. I have by now accumulated a mass of conflicting observations and I think it is better to speak not of 'immobility' but of severely regulated mobility.

Fourthly, I have to admit that the phrase about a country 'without beliefs, without traditions, without culture' was written in the heat of the moment. Russia has always had, and has, traditions, faith and culture; it is just that, for some strange reason, she tries either to repudiate them utterly or, on the contrary, to fence herself off with them from the rest of the world.

Fifthly, I think I was a little premature with my dates. On the one hand I underestimated the Soviet leadership's flexibility; on the other, I overestimated the pace of development of China's stockpiles of nuclear and conventional weapons.

'Détente', Western economic aid and 'letting off steam' by allowing restricted emigration are enabling the Soviet leadership to prolong the quasi-stability of the regime. After five years of post-Khrushchev 'freeze' the regime has switched once again to a moderate foreign policy 'thaw'. Admittedly, as in the fifties, it is the West more than the USSR itself that is melting under this 'thaw'.

However, even with the assistance of Western supporters of 'détente', the stability the Soviet regime maintains is only a sham. The movement of history cannot be halted, and true stability is conscious movement onwards, not being forced to stand shuffling on the spot.

Nor do Western advocates of 'détente' quite understand the connection that exists in Russia between foreign expansion and internal stability. Expansion, which for the Russian philosophers assumes the aspect of Messianism, is Russia's historical *raison d'être*. The moment her expansionist efforts are dealt a severe blow, as, for instance, in the Crimean or Russo-Japanese War, reforms or revolution follow. Successful expansion, on the contrary, somehow neutralizes failures at home. Thus, for instance, success in Angola not only offset the bad harvest in 1975 but even credited the regime with an overall balance in its favour.

I was a little premature with my dates, but I had correctly noted the trends. The regime still has two ways out: either gradual liberalization or a turn towards a nationalist dictatorship, some kind of Russian Nazism, perhaps under the leadership of the military.

The army, unless put to energetic use abroad, constitutes an enormous latent threat inside the country. The fact that for the first time a civilian and not a military man has been appointed Minister of Defence[1]* and that simultaneously the head of the Communist Party together with the new minister were given the rank of Marshal is an indirect pointer to this. However, there are other trends inside the army, as the participation of many officers in opposition to the regime indicates.

Opposition in the USSR – cultural, religious, nationalist and legalist – has survived despite the repression, emigration and 're-pentance' of some of its members. The Democratic Movement, which now calls itself the Movement for Human Rights, has acquired new and forceful supporters. May 1976, for example, saw the founding of the Group for the Promotion of the Observance of the Helsinki Agreements, headed by Professor Yury Orlov.[2]

However, the 'middle class' as a whole is still paralysed by awareness of its own impotence. To the faults of this class which I mentioned in my essay I would like to add one more: lack of culture – culture as a concept including moral values. By and large, 'culture' nowadays is used to mean the command of specific professional skills.

Official art and literature are growing more and more sclerotic. Almost all the most interesting Russian books in the last seven years have been published abroad. Everything more or less interesting that has been published in the USSR has been sanctioned by the authorities for fear that it too may otherwise find its

*Editor's numbers notes may be found on p. 216 ff.

way West. Generally speaking, the existence of an 'unofficial' literature is forcing the authorities to show some indulgence towards those writers who are still with them.

When I was putting the finishing touches to my essay in June 1969 in our little village house – which during my exile was completely destroyed – I hoped that some academic journal would publish it, thereby helping a few dozen Sovietologists somewhat to amplify and clarify their views.

What happened in fact was that the book came out in many languages, in editions running altogether into several hundreds of thousands; thousands of copies were disseminated in the USSR, and in many countries the book is still being bought and read to this day. Of course, I would like to be able to attribute this first and foremost to my literary gift. But I think the fact that the ideas I had expressed were, so to speak, already in the air played a tremendously important role. This is why, incidentally, much of what I first said seven years ago has now become commonplace and why some people may even be at a loss to understand why I speak so meaningfully and significantly of things that everyone had known for donkey's years.

A small boy had to cry, 'But the emperor has no clothes!' in order for everyone to see that the emperor really did have no clothes. I was that small boy.

Some people in Russia have said to me: 'When we read your book seven years ago we thought it was all rubbish and exaggeration, but now we can see you were right.' I have heard the same thing from several Americans, expecially on the subject of Soviet-Chinese-American relations, and I regard it as the highest praise for someone who has attempted to see a few years into the future. The Soviet press first mentioned my book only eight years after its appearance, giving it in its own way high praise: 'One is struck by Amalrik's ability – for all his ignorance of historical questions – to incorporate in so small a compass so much hatred for humanity in general and malice towards the Soviet people in particular.' (*Nedelya*, 20-26 June 1977.) However, the response that most flattered me was the one I heard from an officer of the

KGB, A. V. Pustyakov. 'You hit us below the belt,' he told me, in 1974.

Naturally, not everyone shares this view. Some people, while agreeing with my analysis of Soviet society, are highly sceptical about my prognoses. I realize myself that my forecasts were more in the nature of poetic visions with more emotion than reason at their basis. I recently re-read a short poem which I wrote in 1962, before the thought of writing political pamphlets had ever crossed my mind and when I regarded the Soviet regime as unshakable. I am amazed now how fraught the poem is with the premonition of cataclysms to come and invasion from the East.

I am not alone. Foreboding of retribution from the East is a theme running if not powerfully at least distinctly through Russian philosophical literature. In 1894, ninety years before 1984, the poet Vladimir Solovyov wrote:

> O Rus! Forget thy former glory,
> The double-headed eagle's smashed,
> Thy banners given torn and tattered
> As playthings to the yellow children.

The remaining articles included in this anthology are all connected in one way or another with the original essay. They demonstrate, among other things, that not everyone in the West was prepared to hear the cry that the emperor had no clothes. Some people were more willing to provide the most fantastic explanations, such as that the book had been written on the order of the KGB, than to look at things simply. This is yet further proof of how little the West understands the Soviet Union, a slowly dying yet still monstrously powerful colossus capable of crushing the whole of Europe in the palm of one hand.

In conclusion, it is my duty – and my pleasure – to thank the following persons who assisted me in my work on the book and with the present edition:

Mao Tse-tung, who launched the 'cultural revolution' in China and thereby heightened my interest in Sino-Soviet relations;

Preface to the Second English Edition

Dr Andrei Sakharov, whose article 'Reflections on progress, peaceful coexistence and intellectual freedom' stimulated me to make an indirect reply to him;

Mr Anatole Shub, whose discussions with me helped me to clarify certain of my views;

Dr Vitaly Rubin, who advised me to take the year 1984 for my title, as an allusion to Orwell's book;

Mme Gyuzel Amalrik, my dear wife, whose concern and encouragement made the writing and publication of this book possible;

Mr Yury Maltsev, who read the manuscript and made several valuable comments;

Dr Karel van het Reve, the first person in the West to read the manuscript of the book and concern himself with finding a publisher;

Mr Henry Kamm, who helped me to get my book published in the West; and

Mr Peter Reddaway, who translated it into English.

Andrei Amalrik
1977–8

Will the Soviet Union Survive Until 1984?

I began to express my views about the approaching crisis in the Soviet system in the autumn of 1966, soon after my return to Moscow from exile in Siberia.[1] *At first I discussed these views only with some of my small circle of friends. Then, in November 1967, I set down my thoughts in a letter which I sent to* Literaturnaya Gazeta (Literary Gazette) *and to* Izvestia, *asking them to publish it. Both newspapers politely replied that they would not do so because they could not agree with some of the views I had expressed.*

Nevertheless, subsequent events both in this country and abroad convinced me that many of my assumptions were well founded, and I decided to put them down in an article. At first I thought of entitling it 'Will the Soviet Union Survive Until 1980?' in the belief that 1980 was the nearest likely date in round numbers. In March 1969 a reference to this appeared in the press: the Moscow correspondent of the Washington Post, *Anatole Shub, briefly and not quite accurately described some of my views and cited the title of my article in progress. He referred to me as 'a Russian friend'.**

However, an expert on ancient Chinese thought and an admirer of English literature, to whom I, in turn, must refer only as 'a Russian friend', advised me to change 1980 to 1984. I agreed willingly to the change, expecially since it did not violate my preference for round figures: since it is now 1969, we are looking forward to a time exactly fifteen years hence.

My work on the article was somewhat hampered and delayed by a search of my apartment on 7 May 1969, during which

---

**International Herald Tribune,* 31 March 1969 (Washington *Post,* 15 June 1969).

certain books and documents necessary to the work were taken from me. Still, I consider it my pleasant duty to thank the agents of the KGB and the public prosecutor's office, who carried out the search, for not taking the manuscript of this article and thus making it possible for me to bring the work to a successful end.

Since I regard the conclusions reached here as in many respects debatable, I shall be grateful for constructive criticism.

I have undertaken this study for three compelling reasons.

The first is simply my interest in Russian history. Almost ten years ago, I wrote a work on Kievan Rus.[2] Due to circumstances beyond my control, however, I was forced to interrupt my researches on the origin of the Imperial Russian State; now, as a historian, I hope to be compensated for that loss by being a witness to the end of that state.

Second, I have been able to observe closely the efforts to create an independent social movement in the Soviet Union – a development that in itself is very interesting and deserves at least a preliminary assessment.

And third, I have been hearing and reading a great deal about the so-called 'liberalization' of Soviet society. This idea may be formulated as follows: The situation is better now than it was ten years ago; therefore ten years from now it will be better still. I will attempt to show here why I disagree with this notion.

I must emphasize that my essay is based not on scholarly research but only on observation and reflection. From an academic point of view, it may appear to be only empty chatter. But for Western students of the Soviet Union, at any rate, this discussion should have the same interest that a fish would have for an ichthyologist if it suddenly began to talk.

I

It would appear that in the course of approximately five years, from 1952 to 1957, a kind of 'revolution at the top' took place in our country. This revolution passed through such moments of intense strain as the creation of the so-called enlarged Presidium of the Central Committee of the Communist Party of the Soviet Union,[3] the 'Doctors' Plot',[4] the mysterious death of Stalin, the abolition of the enlarged Presidium, the purge of the state security organs, the mass rehabilitation of political prisoners and the public condemnation of Stalin, and the Polish and Hungarian crises of 1956. It ended with the complete victory of Khrushchev.

Throughout this period the country passively awaited its fate. While struggle was going on continuously 'at the top', not a single voice 'from below' was heard challenging the orders which at any given moment were handed down 'from above'. In actual fact, underground groups with opposition programmes had already begun to appear – for example, the Krasnopevtsev group, which was arrested in 1956.[5] But because they were illegal and received no publicity, each group's protest actions were known only to its handful of members.

But the 'revolution at the top' apparently loosened up the monolithic system created by Stalin and thus made possible some movement in Soviet society. Before the period was over, a new force, independent of the government, began to take shape. It may roughly be called the 'Cultural Opposition'.

Certain writers who until then had swum only in official waters or simply remained silent began speaking with new voices, and some of their works began to be published or were circulated in manuscript. There appeared on the scene many young poets, musicians, artists and writers of satirical lyrics who sang their own songs. Typewritten magazines began to circulate, semi-legal art exhibitions were held and troupes of young actors, singers and entertainers were organized.*

*Examples that come to mind are the publication of *Doctor Zhivago* by Boris Pasternak, the publication of the typewritten magazine *Syntax*[6] by Alexander Ginzburg, the public reading of poems in Moscow's Maiakovsky Square, exhibitions of independent artists like Anatoly Zverev and Oskar Rabin, the official publication of several novels, stories and poems that were later severely criticized, and the appearance of many singers and song-writers like Okudzhava, Galich, Vysotsky and others whose songs circulated in millions of tape recordings. All were manifestations of widely differing levels of culture, but all were directed against 'official' culture.

This movement was directed not against the political regime as such but only against its culture, which the regime regarded as a component part of itself. Therefore the regime began to combat the Cultural Opposition, winning complete victory in case after case. Writers 'repented', publishers of underground magazines were arrested, art exhibitions were closed and poets were dispersed.

Nevertheless, victory over the Cultural Opposition as a whole was not achieved. On the contrary, the opposition was to some extent gradually absorbed into official art, its own nature being modified in the process; but by modifying official art in turn, it was able to preserve some of its identity as a cultural phenomenon. At the same time, by reconciling itself to the existence of a Cultural Opposition and virtually ignoring it, the regime robbed it of the political impact it had acquired as a result of the official struggle against it.

At this time, however, a new force emerged from within the Cultural Opposition; a force that stood not only against official culture but against many aspects of the ideology and practice of the regime. It emerged as a result of the crossing of two opposing trends: the striving of society to obtain greater social and political information and the efforts of the regime to control even more completely every aspect of information given to the public.

This new force came to be known as 'samizdat'.* Novels, stories, plays, memoirs, articles, open letters, leaflets, shorthand records of official meetings and court hearings in dozens, hun-

---

Samizdat refers to work that is published by the author himself, and it is, in fact, a traditional Russian method of circumventing official censorship. Examples of present-day *samizdat* are the novels of Alexander Solzhenitsyn, the memoirs about life in prison camps of Yevgenia Ginzburg,[7] Olga Adamova and Anatoly Marchenko,[8] the articles of Anatoly Krasnov-Levitin,[9] the short stories of Varlaam Shalamov, the poems of Natalya Gorbanyevskaya,[10] and others. But it should be noted that a significant proportion of *samizdat* is anonymous. *Samizdat* also includes works that have been published abroad and were only later brought into the Soviet Union, such as the books of Andrei Siniavsky[11] and Yuli Daniel,[12] as well as books of foreign authors which have been either typed out or put on microfilm. Examples are the writings of George Orwell and Milovan Djilas and articles from foreign newspapers and magazines.

17

dreds and thousands of typewritten copies and photostats began to circulate throughout the country.

Gradually, over a period of perhaps five years, the emphasis of *samizdat* shifted from literary to documentary works and acquired a steadily more pronounced social and political content. Naturally, the regime recognized *samizdat* as potentially more dangerous than the Cultural Opposition, and therefore it fights it with even greater vigour.

Examples of this struggle include the sentencing of Siniavsky and Daniel to seven and five years, respectively, of imprisonment in 'strict-regime' labour camps for having published their books abroad (1965),[13] the sentencing of Viacheslav Chornovil to three years for compiling an account of political trials in the Ukraine (1967),[14] the sentencing of Yuri Galanskov to seven years for compiling the anthology *Phoenix*,[15] the sentencing of Alexander Ginzburg to five years for compiling a collection of documents on the trial of Siniavsky and Daniel (1968),[16] and the sentencing of Anatoly Marchenko to one year after he wrote his book on the prison camps of the post-Stalin era (1968).*

Nevertheless, *samizdat*, like the Cultural Opposition, gradually gave birth to a new, independent force which can already be regarded as a real political opposition to the regime or, at least, as a political opposition in embryo. This has turned into a social movement that calls itself the Democratic Movement. It can be regarded as a new phase in the opposition to the regime, and as a *political* opposition, for the following reasons:

First, although it has not adopted a definite organizational form, it regards itself as a movement and calls itself such, it has leaders and activists, and it relies on a considerable number of sympathizers. Second, it consciously sets itself specific aims and

---

*Severe measures are also taken against those who circulate the works of *samizdat*. For instance, the typist Vera Lashkova was sentenced to one year together with Ginzburg and Galanskov merely for having typed their manuscripts. Yuri Gendler, Lev Kvachevsky and Anatoly Studenkov were sentenced, respectively, to four years, three years and one year (in Leningrad) for reading and circulating literature that had not been passed by the censors (1968), and Ilia Burmistrovich was sentenced to three years (in Moscow) for the same offence (1969).

chooses particular tactics, although these are still diffuse. Third, it desires legal status and publicity for its activities, and works hard for such publicity. In this it differs from the small or even large underground groups.*

Before examining to what extent the Democratic Movement is a mass movement and how well defined and attainable its aims are – that is, whether it is really a movement and whether it has any chances of success – it is worth examining the ideological foundations on which any opposition in the Soviet Union can be based.

Of course, as the author himself clearly remembers, even in 1952–6 there were a great number of people who were dissatisfied with the regime and opposed to it. But not only was this discontent of a drawing-room character; it also leaned heavily on a negative ideology: the regime was bad because it did or did not do this or that. The question of what was desirable was generally not asked. It was also assumed either that the regime was not living up to the ideology it professed or that the ideology itself was worthless. The search for a positive ideology forceful enough to oppose the official ideology did not begin until the end of this period.

This is a very interesting question, and my view of it may be mistaken since I do not know the full facts. For very obvious reasons it is simply impossible to know them. They will become known only with the publication of the post-war archives of the KGB. I do not intend to suggest that there were no individuals, or even small groups, who had definite and positive ideologies. However, there prevailed at the time such extreme spiritual iso-

---

*Details about several groups of this sort have, despite the secrecy which surrounded their trials, become known since 1956: the group of Krasno-pevtsev and Rendel, which was tried in 1956; the group of Osipov and Kuznetsov (1961); the group that published the magazine *Kolokol* (*The Bell*) in Leningrad (1964); the group of Dergunov (1967); and others. The largest of the underground organizations so far exposed has been the All-Russian Social-Christian Union for the Liberation of the People. Twenty-one members of this group were sentenced in Leningrad in 1967–8, although the Union's total membership was far greater.

lation, such a total absence of publicity and of the faintest hope for the possibility of change, that the chance of any positive ideologies developing was virtually destroyed at the start.

It can be said that over the course of the last fifteen years at least three ideological viewpoints on which opposition is founded have begun to crystallize. They are 'genuine Marxism-Leninism', 'Christian ideology' and 'liberal ideology'.

'Genuine Marxism–Leninism' contends that the regime, having perverted Marxist–Leninist ideology for its own purposes, does not practise real Marxism–Leninism, and that in order to cure the ills of our society it is essential to return to the true principles of that doctrine.

Supporters of 'Christian ideology' maintain that the life of society must return to Christian moral principles, which are interpreted in a somewhat Slavophile spirit, with a claim for a special role for Russia.

Finally, believers in 'liberal ideology' ultimately envisage a transition to a Western kind of democratic society, which would, however, retain the principle of public or governmental ownership of the means of production.

Representatives of 'Marxist-Leninist ideology' include Alexei Kosterin, who died in 1968, Peter Grigorenko and Ivan Yakhimovich.[17] 'Christian ideology' was the inspiration behind the All-Russian Social-Christian Union, whose most notable figure was I. Ogurtsov.* Finally, Pavel Litvinov[18] and, with some reservations, Academician Andrei Sakharov[19] can be considered representatives of 'liberal ideology'. It is an interesting fact that all these ideologies have, in modified form, also penetrated circles close to the regime.

These ideologies are, however, largely amorphous. No one has yet defined them with sufficient completeness and persuasiveness. Very often they are merely taken for granted by their adherents.

*I want to make especially clear that by what I have tentatively called 'Christian ideology' I mean a political doctrine and not a religious philosophy or an ecclesiastical ideology, representatives of which would be more correctly regarded as members of the Cultural Opposition.

The followers of each doctrine assume that they all believe in something in common, but what that is exactly no one knows. Moreover, these doctrines have no clear limits and often overlap each other. And even in their amorphous forms, they are believed in by only a small group of people. Yet there are many signs that among the broad masses, especially among the working class, the need is felt for an ideology that can serve as a base for a negative attitude towards the regime and its official doctrine.*

The Democratic Movement, so far as I am aware, includes representatives of all three of the ideologies that I have described. Its own ideology, therefore, may either be an eclectic fusion of 'genuine Marxism-Leninism', Russian Christianity and liberalism, or it may base itself on the common elements in these ideologies (as they are interpreted in the USSR today). Evidently the latter is what is happening. Although the Democratic Movement is in its formative period and has no clearly defined programme, all its supporters assume at least one common aim: the rule of law, founded on respect for the basic rights of man.

The number of supporters of the movement is almost as indeterminable as its aim. They amount to several dozen active participants and several hundred who sympathize with the movement and give it their support. It would be impossible to give an exact number, not only because it is unknown but also because it is constantly changing. Now, when the regime is 'escalating repression', the movement will probably go into decline – some of its members will go to prison and others will sever their

---

*This is particularly apparent in some of the letters from Soviet citizens received by Pavel Litvinov in reply to the open letter addressed by himself and Larisa Bogoraz-Daniel 'To World Public Opinion'[20] during the Galanskov–Ginzburg trial and published in the West by Professor Karel van het Reve.[21]

But perhaps the clearest example is provided by Anatoly Marchenko in his book *My Testimony*. As an ordinary labourer, with seven years' education, he was sent to prison camp on a trumped-up political charge. There, in search of an ideological grounding, he read through the entire thirty-odd volumes of the works of Lenin. (Apparently this was the only political literature in the camp library.)

connections with it. However, as soon as the pressure subsides, the number of members will probably rise rapidly.

More interesting, perhaps, than the number of its supporters is the social composition of the movement. The following analysis is based on a representative sample: those who protested against the trial of Galanskov and Ginzburg.

In essence, the trial served as an occasion for public opinion to voice demands that the regime pay greater respect to the rule of law and to human rights. The majority of those who signed protests against the trial[22] did not even know Galanskov or Ginzburg personally. Thus the vigorous and extensive public protests against the violations of legality at this trial can probably be considered the beginning of the movement.

It can be said therefore to have begun in 1968. But even earlier, at least from 1965, there had been attempts at mass action on behalf of legality. Such were the demonstration of 5 December 1965 in Pushkin Square in Moscow which demanded a public trial for Siniavsky and Daniel (about one hundred persons participated, no arrests were made, but a group of students was expelled from Moscow University); collective letters to various government agencies in 1966 seeking clemency for Siniavsky and Daniel,[23] a collective letter against efforts to rehabilitate Stalin and one protesting the new articles of the Criminal Code (190/1 and 190/3),[24] both of which were signed by prominent representatives of the intelligentsia (their prominence was evidently what forestalled any significant repressive action against the signers); a demonstration on 22 January 1967 in Pushkin Square to demand the liberation of Yuri Galanskov, Alexei Dobrovolsky, Vera Lashkova and Peter Radzievsky, who had been arrested several days earlier (about thirty persons participated, five were arrested and four sentenced to terms of one to three years' imprisonment under the newly approved Article 190/3 of the Criminal Code).[25]

All told, 738 people signed their names to the various collective or individual letters of protest against the Ginzburg–Galanskov trial. The professions of thirty-eight of them are unknown. The following is a compilation of those whose professions are known:

Occupation	Per cent*
Academics	45
People engaged in the arts	22
Engineers and technical specialists	13
Publishing-house employees, teachers, doctors and lawyers	9
Workers	6
Students	5

If we accept this social composition of the signers of letters of protest as typical, it is clear that the basic support of the movement comes from academic circles. Yet, because of the nature of their work, their position in our society and their way of thinking, scholars seem to me to be those least capable of purposeful action. They are very willing to 'reflect' but extremely reluctant to act. It appears to me that scholarly work requires, in general, special exertion and total concentration. The privileged position of scholars in society militates against their taking risks, and the

*In absolute figures, this is the breakdown:

Occupation	Number
Academics	314
(holders of doctorates, 35; holders of the intermediate degree of 'candidate', 94; without higher degree, 185)	
People in the arts	157
(members of the official unions, 90; non-members, 67)	
Engineers and technical specialists	92
(engineers, 80; technical specialists, 12)	
Publishing-house employees, teachers, doctors and lawyers	65
(editors, 14; other publishing employees, 14; teachers, 15; doctors, 9; lawyers, 3; retired members of these professions, 7; masters of sport, 1; priests, 1; chairmen of collective farms, 1)	
Workers	40
Students	32

These figures may not be completely reliable and are therefore approximate. I have taken them from *The Trial of the Four*, a collection of documents on the trial of Galanskov, Ginzburg, Dobrovolsky and Lashkova, which was compiled and annotated by Pavel Litvinov.[26] I counted each signer only once, regardless of how many statements and protests he signed. I think that if we counted the persons who signed *all* the statements and letters demanding adherence to the laws, beginning with the letters written during the trial of Siniavsky and Daniel in 1966 and ending with the protests against the arrest of General Peter G. Grigorenko in 1969, the number of signers would be found to surpass 1,000 (people, not signatures).

kind of thinking acquired through scholarly work has a more speculative than pragmatic character. Although at present workers represent a more conservative and passive group than scholars, I can easily imagine, some years from now, large-scale strikes in factories, but I cannot visualize a strike in any scientific research institute.

Further, it is clear that in broader terms the basic support for the movement comes from the intelligentsia. But since this word is too vague, defining not so much the position in society of a person, or a given social group, as the ability of members of this group to perform intellectual work, it would be better if I used the term 'middle class'.

Actually, we know that in all countries persons of higher-than-average income who practise professions that call for considerable preparation require a certain measure of pragmatic and intellectual freedom for their activities. Furthermore, like any property-owning class, they can only function under the rule of law. They are, consequently, the basic stratum of any society on which a democratic regime bases itself. I believe that the gradual formation of such a class is taking place in our country. It can also be described as the 'class of specialists'.

In order to exist and carry out its activities, the regime was obliged throughout the post-war period to encourage the country's economy and scientific resources. Since the new scientific and technical personnel are taking on more and more of a mass character in contemporary society, it is they who have bred this sizeable class.

Its members have gained for themselves and their families a standard of living that is relatively high by Soviet standards – regular good food, attractive clothes, a nicely furnished cooperative apartment, sometimes even a car and, of course, available entertainment. They pursue professions that assure them a position of respect in society. They achieve a certain level of culture, for instance, opportunities to listen to serious music, to become interested in art or to go regularly to the theatre. They possess the ability to assess more or less accurately their own position and the position of society as a whole.

This group includes people in liberal professions, such as writers or actors, those occupied in academic or academic-administrative work, the managerial group in the economic field and so on. They are, as I have said, a 'class of specialists'. Obviously, this class is beginning to become conscious of its unity and to make its presence felt.

This, too, becomes apparent from an analysis of the authors and signers of the various protests and petitions against the trial of Galanskov and Ginzburg. I do not suggest, of course, that the *entire* 'middle class' rose to the defence of the two 'renegades' but that *some* representatives of that class have already come to realize clearly the need for the rule of law and have begun, at personal risk, to demand it from the regime.

Thus there exists an influential class, or stratum of society, on which the Democratic Movement could seemingly base itself. But there are at least three interrelated factors that militate strongly against such a development.

Two of these factors spring to mind immediately. First, the planned elimination from society of the most independent-minded and active of its members, which has been going on for decades, has left an imprint of greyness and mediocrity on all strata of society – and this could not fail to be reflected in the 'middle class' which is once again taking shape. This elimination, whether through emigration or exile from the country or through imprisonment or physical annihilation, has affected all strata of our people.

Second, that section of the 'middle class' which most clearly recognizes the need for democratic reforms is also the section that is most imbued with the defensive thought, 'Well, there's nothing I can do anyway' or 'You can't break down the wall by beating your head against it.' In reaction to the power of the regime, it practises a cult of its own impotence.

The third factor, although less obvious, is most interesting. As is well known, in any country the stratum of society least inclined towards change or any sort of independent action is that composed of state employees. This is natural, because every government worker considers himself too insignificant in comparison with the power apparatus of which he is only a small cog to demand of that apparatus any kind of change. At the same time, he has been relieved of all social responsibility, since his job is simply to carry out orders. Thus he always has the feeling of having performed his duty even though he had done things that he would not have done had he been given a choice.

(On the other hand, the person who issues the orders is equally freed from a sense of responsibility inasmuch as the officials on the level beneath him regard his orders as 'good' because they come from above. This creates the illusion among the authorities that everything they do is good.)

For the government worker, the notion of work is narrowed to the notion of a 'job'. He is an automaton at his post and passive when he leaves it. The government worker's psychology is therefore the one that is most convenient both for the government and for himself.

In our country, since all of us work for the state, we all have the psychology of government workers. Writers who are members of the Union of Writers, scholars employed in government institutions, common labourers or collective farmers are creatures of this psychology just as much as are officials of the KGB or the Ministry of the Interior.

Therefore, much of the overt and covert protest in the Soviet Union has the character of the dissatisfaction of a junior clerk with the attitude of his superior. This can be seen clearly in the attitude of a number of writers whose names are used in the West as yardsticks of 'Soviet liberalism'. They are inclined to regard their rights and duties not so much as the rights and duties of a *writer* as those of an 'official in the literary department', to use the expression of a character in Dostoyevsky.

For example, after Alexander Solzhenitsyn wrote his famous letter about the situation of the Soviet writer,[27] the Moscow correspondent of the *Daily Telegraph* of London, John Miller, asked a well-known Soviet poet in a private conversation whether he intended to join in Solzhenitsyn's protest. The poet said no.

'You must understand,' he said, 'this is our internal affair, a question of our relations with the state.'

In other words, he regarded the matter not as a question of the writer's conscience and his moral right and duty to write what he thinks, but as a question of internal relations within the Soviet 'literary department'. He may also protest, but in the manner of a petty clerk, not against the 'department' as such but against his rather low salary or against his rude boss. Naturally, this is an 'internal matter' and should be of no interest to those who do not belong to the 'department'.

This curious conversation took place in one of the shops in Moscow where those privileged to have foreign currency are allowed to buy goods not available on the Soviet market.

It goes without saying that the 'middle class' is no exception in adopting this government-employee attitude; indeed, this psychology is particularly typical of it by virtue of its position in the middle of the social scale. Many members of this class are simply functionaries of the Communist Party or governmental apparatus. They regard the regime as a lesser evil than the painful process of changing it.

Consequently we are faced with an interesting phenomenon. Although there exists in our country a social class capable of comprehending the principles of personal freedom, rule of law and democratic government, a class that needs those principles and provides the emerging Democratic Movement with its basic contingent of supporters, the vast majority of this class is so mediocre, its ways of thinking are so much those of the government employee, and its intellectually most independent members are so passive that the success of a Democratic Movement based on it seems to be to be gravely in doubt.

It must be said, however, that this 'paradox of the middle class' is connected in a curious way with a 'paradox of the regime'. We are aware that the regime underwent very dynamic internal changes in the five years before the war.[28] However, the subsequent regeneration of the bureaucratic élite was carried out by the retention of those who were most obedient and unquestioning. This bureaucratic method of 'unnatural selection' of the most obedient members of the old bureaucracy, together with the

27

elimination from the ruling caste of the boldest and most independent-minded, created over the years an increasingly weaker
and more indecisive generation of élite. Accustomed to obey un-
conditionally and without thought in order to attain power,
bureaucrats, once they have attained that power, are very good at
holding on to it but have no idea how to use it. Not only are they
incapable of conceiving new ideas; they regard any novel
thought as an assault on their own prerogatives.

Evidently we have reached the sad point where the idea of
power is no longer connected with either a doctrine, the personality of a leader or a tradition, but only with power itself.
Every governmental institution and position is sustained by no
other force than the realization that it is an essential part of the
existing system.

Naturally, self-preservation is bound to be the only aim of
such a regime, at least in its domestic policy. This has come to
mean the self-preservation of the bureaucratic élite. In order to
remain in power, the regime must change and evolve, but in
order to preserve itself, everything must remain unchanged. The
contradiction can be noted particularly in the case of the 'economic reform', which is being carried out so slowly and yet is so
vital to the regime.[29]

Self-preservation is clearly the dominant drive. The regime
wants neither to 'restore Stalinism' nor to 'persecute the intelligentsia' nor to ' render fraternal assistance' to those who have not
asked for it, like Czechoslovakia. The only thing it wants is for
everything to go on as before: authorities to be recognized, the
intelligentsia to keep quiet, no rocking of the system by dangerous and unfamiliar reforms.

The regime is not on the attack but on the defence. Its motto
is: 'Don't touch us and we won't touch you.' Its aim: Let everything be as it was. This is probably the most humane objective the
regime has set for itself in the last half-century, but it is also the
least appealing.

Thus we have a passive bureaucratic élite opposed to a passive
'middle class'. Moreover, however passive the élite is, it really

does not need to make any changes, and in theory it could remain in power for a very long time, getting away with only the slightest concessions and minor measures of repression.

It is clear that a regime in such a quasi-stable condition required a definite legal framework, based either on a tacit understanding by all members of society of what is required of them or on written law. In the days of Stalin and even of Khrushchev, there was a sense of direction emanating from above and felt by all, which guided every official unerringly to an awareness of what was currently required of him (reinforced, however, by special instructions) and enabled everyone else to sense what was expected of him. At the same time there existed a 'décor' of laws from which the authorities chose whatever they needed at any given moment. But gradually, both 'from above' and 'from below', a desire became noticeable for more stable 'written' norms rather than this 'tacit understanding'. This desire created a rather uncertain situation.

The necessity for a modicum of the rule of law had made itself felt 'at the top' earlier, during the period when the role of the state security organs was being curbed and mass rehabilitations were taking place. In the decade beginning in 1954, gradual, though very slow, progress was achieved in the fields both of formal legislation and of the practical implementation of the laws. This took the form of the signing of a number of international conventions and of an attempt to bring Soviet law into some kind of harmony with international legal norms. Furthermore, personnel changes were carried out among investigative and judicial authorities.

This very slow movement towards the rule of law was further retarded by the following factors: First, the authorities, for various reasons of current policy, issued decrees and regulations which directly contradicted the international conventions they had just signed as well as the approved principles of Soviet law. For example, the decree ordering five years of exile and forced labour for persons with no fixed employment, which was approved in 1961, was not made part of the Criminal Code. Then there was the decree which increased the penalty for illegal currency dealing to include death and which was given *de facto* retroactive force.

Second, the personnel changes were carried out on a very limited scale and with little consistency. They were hampered by a shortage of administrative officials who understood the concept of the rule of law.

Third, the professional egotism of the administrative officials led them to oppose anything that might lessen their influence or abolish their privileged position in society.

Fourth, the very idea of the rule of law had virtually no roots in Soviet society and was in blatant conflict with the officially proclaimed doctrines about the 'class' approach to all phenomena.[30]

While the movement towards the rule of law, which had begun 'from the top', thus gradually bogged down in a bureaucratic swamp, suddenly voices demanding the observance of the laws were heard 'from below'. And, indeed, the 'middle class' – the only class in Soviet society to understand and to feel the need for the rule of law – had begun, albeit very timidly, to demand that it be treated not in accordance with the current requirements of the regime but on a 'legal basis'.

It now became evident that in Soviet law there exists, if I may use the term, a broad 'grey belt' – activities that the law does not formally forbid but which are, in fact, forbidden in practice – for instance: contacts between Soviet citizens and foreigners; a concern over non-Marxist philosophies or art inconsistent with the notions of socialist realism; attempts to put out typewritten literary collections; spoken or written criticism not of the system as a whole, which is forbidden under Articles 70 and 190/1 of the Criminal Code, but of particular institutions within the system.

Thus two trends are evident today: the efforts of the regime to 'blacken' the grey belt – by means of amendments to the Criminal Code, trials designed to serve as examples to others, and instructions to administrative officials on how to enforce existing regulations – and an effort by the 'middle class' to 'whiten' the belt, simply by doing things that had earlier been considered impossible and constantly referring to their lawfulness.

All this places the regime in a rather awkward situation, particularly if one bears in mind that the idea of the rule of law will begin to take hold in other strata of society. On the one hand the regime, in the interests of stability, is constantly forced to observe its own laws, while on the other it is constantly forced to violate them so as to counteract the tendency towards democratization.

This has given rise to two interesting phenomena: mass persecution outside the judicial system and selective judicial persecution. Non-judicial persecution is exemplified primarily by dismissals from work and expulsions from the party. In the course of one month, for instance, over fifteen per cent of all those who had signed petitions demanding observance of the law in connection with the trial of Galanskov and Ginzburg were dismissed from their jobs, and almost all those who were party members were expelled from the party.

Selective judicial persecution has the aim of frightening those who might be liable for trial on the same charges. Thus it may happen that persons who have committed a more serious crime – from the regime's point of view – may be allowed to go free, while persons who have committed a lesser infraction may be thrown into prison if this requires less expenditure of bureaucratic effort or the circumstances of the moment make it more desirable.

A typical example was the trial of the Moscow engineer, Irina Belogorodskaya, in January 1969. She was accused of 'attempting to circulate' what the court held to be an 'anti-Soviet' appeal in defence of the political prisoner Anatoly Marchenko and was sentenced to one year's imprisonment. At the same time, the authors of the appeal, who publicly acknowledged that they had written and circulated it, were not even called as witnesses.

Another contemptible repressive measure is becoming increasingly widespread – forcible commitment to psychiatric hospitals. This is done in the case both of persons who are completely sane and of those with slight mental disorders who do not need hospitalization or compulsory treatment.

As we can now see, the existence of a 'Stalinism without violence', while calming the fears of the people which date from the previous era of violence, inevitably produces a new kind of violence: first, 'selective persecution' of malcontents, then 'lenient' mass persecution. And what next?

Still, looking back over the last fifteen years, we observe that the process of regularizing the legal system had advanced, slowly but rather steadily, and has gone so far that it will be difficult to reverse it by the customary bureaucratic methods. It is a moot point whether this process represents part of the liberalization of the regime which is – or at least was until recently – supposed to be taking place in our country. After all, it is well known that the evolution of our state and society has gone forward not only in the field of law but also in the economy, in culture and in other areas.

In fact, not only does every Soviet citizen feel that he is living in greater security and enjoying more personal freedom than he did fifteen years ago, but the director of an industrial enterprise now has the right to decide for himself matters that previously were not his to decide, while the writer or theatre director works within much wider limits than he did before. The same can be said about almost every area of life in our country. This has given rise to yet another ideology in our society, possibly the most widespread one; it can be called the 'ideology of reformism'.

It is based on the view that a certain 'humanization of socialism' will take place and that the inert and oppressive system will be replaced by a dynamic and liberal one. This will be achieved through gradual changes and piecemeal reforms, as well as by replacing the old bureaucratic élite with a more intelligent and more reasonable group. In other words, this theory is based on the belief that 'Reason will prevail' and that 'Everything will be all right.'

This is why it is so popular in academic circles and, in general, among those who are not badly off even now and who therefore hope that others will also come to accept the view that it is better to be well fed and free than to be hungry and enslaved. I think that all the American hopes about the Soviet Union are derived from this naïve point of view. We know, however, that history, and Russian history in particular, has by no means been a continuous victory for reason and that the whole history of mankind has not followed an unbroken line of progress.

I would like to illustrate this with a small but typical incident involving my friend Anatole Shub, the former Moscow correspondent of the Washington *Post*. At the end of March 1969 he told me that in his opinion the situation of the regime was so complicated and difficult that in all likelihood there would be a plenary meeting of the Central Committee of the Communist Party in April. At this meeting, even if no decisive changes were made in the party leadership, at least a new, more moderate and more reasonable policy course would be adopted.

Therefore, he intended to behave with maximum caution before the meeting, so as to avoid being the last American correspondent to be expelled from Moscow before the liberal changes occurred. However, no changes were made in April – if the changes in the leadership in Czechoslovakia are excluded – and Anatole Shub was expelled from Moscow in May.

Of course, Anatole Shub is one of the Americans who best understands Soviet reality, and he may possibly have had some reason for believing that there would be a plenum in April. However, he, too, held the exaggerated American belief in 'reasonable changes', which are obviously possible only where life is based fundamentally, even if only partially, on reasonable foundations.

In addition to this faith in reason, Americans apparently also believe that the gradual improvement in the standard of living, as well as the spread of Western culture and ways of life, will gradually transform Soviet society – that foreign tourists, jazz records and mini-skirts will help to create a 'humane socialism'. It is possible that we will indeed have a 'socialism' with bare knees someday, but not likely one with a human face.[31]

In my view, the growth of material conveniences of everyday life and economic well-being does not in itself prevent or eliminate oppression. As an example, one may cite such a developed country as Nazi Germany. Oppression is always oppression, but

33

in each country it has its own specific traits, and we can correctly understand the causes that brought it about and that can lead to its elimination only in the historical context of that country.

In my opinion, the trouble lies not so much in the fact that the degree of freedom available to us is minimal as compared with that needed for a developed society, and that the process of liberalization, instead of being steadily accelerated, is at times palpably slowed down, perverted or turned back, as in the fact that the very nature of the process gives us grounds to doubt its ultimate success.

It would seem that liberalization presupposes some kind of purposeful plan, put into effect gradually 'from above' through reforms and other measures, to adapt our system to contemporary conditions and lead it to a radical regeneration. As we know, there has been, and still is, no such plan, and no radical reforms have been, or are being, carried out. There are only isolated and uncoordinated attempts at emergency repairs by tinkering in various ways with the bureaucratic machine.

The so-called 'economic reform', of which I have already spoken, is in essence a half-measure and is in practice being sabotaged by the party machine, because if such a reform were carried to its logical end, it would threaten the power of the machine.

Liberalization could, however, take a 'spontaneous' form. It could come as the result of constant concessions on the part of the regime to the demands of a society that had its own plan for liberalization, and of constant efforts by the regime to adapt itself to the storm of changing conditions all over the world. In other words, the system would be self-regulating: difficulties in foreign and domestic policy, economic troubles, etc., would constantly forewarn the ruling élite of changing conditions.

We find, however, that even this is not the case. The regime considers itself the acme of perfection and therefore has no wish to change its ways either of its own free will or, still less, by making concessions to anyone or anything.

The current process of 'widening the area of freedom' could be more aptly described as the growing decrepitude of the regime.

The regime is simply growing old and can no longer suppress everyone and everything with the same strength and vigour as before; the composition of the élite is changing, as we have mentioned; the contemporary world, in which the regime is already finding it very hard to keep its bearings, is becoming more complex; and the structure of society is changing.

We can visualize all this in the following allegory: A man is standing in a tense posture, his hands raised above his head. Another, in an equally strained pose, holds a Tommy gun to the first man's stomach. Naturally, they cannot stand like this for very long. The second man will get tired and loosen his grip on the gun, and the first will take advantage of this to lower his hands and relax a bit. In just this way, we are now witnessing a growing yearning for a quiet life and for comfort – even a kind of 'comfort cult' – on all levels of our society, particularly at the top and in the middle.

If however, one views the present 'liberalization' as the growing decripitude of the regime rather than its regeneration, then the logical result will be its death, which will be followed by anarchy.

If, furthermore, one regards the evolution of the regime as analogous to the growth of entropy,[32] then the Democratic Movement, which I analysed at the beginning of this study, could be considered an anti-entropic phenomenon. One may, of course, hope – and this will probably come true – that the emerging movement will succeed, despite persecution, in becoming influential, will work out a sufficiently concrete programme, will find the structure necessary to its goals and attract many followers. But at the same time, I think that its base in society – the 'middle class', or, more exactly, a part of the 'middle class' – is too weak and too beset by internal contradictions to allow the movement to engage in a real face-to-face struggle with the regime or, in the event of the regime's self-destruction or its collapse as a result of mass disorders, to become a force capable of reorganizing society in a new way. But will the Democratic Movement perhaps be able to find a broader base of support among the masses?

Will the Soviet Union Survive Until 1984?

It is very hard to answer this question, if only because no one, not even the bureaucratic élite, knows exactly what attitudes prevail among the wider sections of the population. The KGB, of course, supplies the bureaucratic élite with information, gathered by its special methods, about popular feelings in the country. This information obviously differs from the picture drawn daily in the newspapers. However, one can only guess how true to reality the KGB's information is. It is, incidentally, paradoxical that the regime should devote enormous effort to keep everyone from talking and then waste further effort to learn what people are talking about and what they want.

As I see it, popular views can be described by the words 'passive discontent'. The discontent is directed not against the regime as such – the majority do not think about it, or they feel that there is no alternative – but rather against particular aspects of the regime, aspects which are, nevertheless, essential to its existence.

The workers, for example, are bitter over having no rights *vis-à-vis* the factory management. The collective farmers are resentful about their total dependence on the *kolkhoz* chairman, who, in turn depends entirely on the district administration. Everybody is angered by the great inequalities in wealth, the low wages, the austere housing conditions, the lack of essential consumer goods, compulsory registration at their places of residence and work and so forth.

The discontent is now becoming louder, and some people are beginning to wonder who is actually to blame. The gradual though slow improvement in the standard of living, due largely to intensive housing construction, does not diminish the anger though it does somewhat neutralize it. It is clear, however, that a sharp slowdown, a halt or even a reversal in the improvement of the standard of living would arouse such explosions of anger, mixed with violence, as were never before thought possible.*

Inasmuch as the regime, because of its ossification, will find it increasingly difficult to raise industrial output, it is obvious that the standard of living in many sectors of our society may be

*For this reason, I believe, the regime did not carry out early in 1969 its intention of raising prices sharply on many goods, preferring instead a kind of creeping inflation. The possible consequences of sharp price increases

threatened. What forms will the people's discontent take then? Legitimate democratic resistance or an extreme form of individual or mass acts of violence?

As I see it, no idea can ever be put into practice if it is not understood by a majority of the people. Whether because of its historical traditions or for some other reason, the idea of self-government, of equality before the law and of personal freedom – and the responsibility that goes with these – are almost completely incomprehensible to the Russian people. Even in the idea of pragmatic freedom, a Russian tends to see not so much the possibility of securing a good life for himself as the danger that some clever fellow will make good at his expense.

To the majority of the people the very word 'freedom' is synonymous with 'disorder' or the opportunity to indulge with impunity in some kind of anti-social or dangerous activity. As for respecting the rights of an individual as such, the idea simply arouses bewilderment. One can respect strength, authority, even intellect or education, but it is preposterous to the popular mind that the human personality should represent any kind of value.

As a people, we have not benefited from Europe's humanist tradition. In Russian history man has always been a means and never in any sense an end. It is paradoxical that the term 'period of the cult of the personality' – by which the Stalin era is euphemistically designated – came to mean for us a period of such humiliation and repression of the human personality as even our people had never previously experienced.

Moreover, official propaganda constantly makes the utmost effort to set the notion of the 'communal' against the notion of the 'personal', clearly underlining the insignificance of the latter and the grandeur of the former. Hence, any interest in the 'personal', an interest that is natural and inevitable, has come to be regarded as unnatural and egotistical.

Does this mean that the masses have no positive idea whatever, except the idea of 'strong government' – a government that is right because it is strong and that therefore must on no account

---

were brought home to the regime by the 'hunger riot' in Novocherkassk[33] after Khruschchev raised the prices of meat and dairy products.

weaken? The Russian people, as can be seen from both their past and present history, have at any rate one idea that appears positive: the idea of *justice*. The government that thinks and acts in everything for us must be not only strong but also just. All must live justly and act justly.

It is worth being burnt at the stake for that idea, but not for the right to 'do as you wish'. For despite the apparent attractiveness of the idea of justice, if one examines it closely, one realizes that it represents the most destructive aspect of Russian psychology. In practice, 'justice' involves the desire that 'nobody should live better than I do' (but not a desire for the much-vaunted notion of equalizing wages, since the fact that many people live worse is willingly accepted).

The idea of justice is motivated by hatred of everything that is outstanding, which we make no effort to imitate but, on the contrary, try to bring down to our level, by hatred of any sense of initiative, of any higher or more dynamic way of life than the life we live ourselves. This psychology is, of course, most typical of the peasantry and least typical of the 'middle class'. However, peasants and those of peasant origin constitute the overwhelming majority in our country.

As I have observed myself, many peasants find someone else's success more painful than their own failure. In general, when the average Russian sees that he is living less well than his neighbour, he will concentrate not on trying to do better for himself but rather on trying to bring his neighbour down to his own level. My reasoning may seem naïve to some people, but I have been able to observe scores of examples in both village and town, and I see in this one of the typical traits of the Russian psyche.

Thus two ideas that the masses understand and accept – the idea of force and the idea of justice – are equally inimical to democratic ideas, which are based on individualism. To these must be added three more negative and interrelated factors: first, the continued low cultural level of the greater part of our people, especially in respect to everyday culture; second, the dominance of the many myths assiduously propagated by the mass information media;

and, third, the extreme social disorientation of the bulk of people.

The 'proletarianization' of the countryside has created an 'alien class' – neither peasant nor working class. They have the dual psychology of the owners of tiny homesteads and of farm hands working on gigantic and anonymous farms. How this class views itself, and what it wants, is known, I think, to nobody. Furthermore, the mass exodus of peasants to the city has created a new type of city dweller: a person who has broken with his old environment, way of life and culture and who is finding it very difficult to discover his place in his new environment and feels ill at ease in it. He is both frightened and aggressive. He no longer has any idea to what level of society he belongs.

While the old social structure in both town and village has been completely destroyed, a new one is only just beginning to form. The 'ideological foundations' on which it is being built are extremely primitive: the desire for material well-being (relatively modest from a Western viewpoint) and the instinct for self-preservation. Thus the concept 'profitable' is confronted with the concept 'risky'.

It is hard to tell whether, aside from those purely material criteria, the bulk of our people possess any kind of moral criteria – such as 'honourable' and 'dishonourable', 'good' and 'bad', 'right' and 'wrong', the supposedly eternal principles which function as inhibiting and guiding factors when the mechanism of social constraint begins to fall apart and man is left to his own devices.

I have formed the impression, which may be wrong, that our people do not have any such moral criteria – or hardly any. The Christian ethic, with its concepts of right and wrong, has been shaken loose and driven out of the popular consciousness. An attempt was made to replace it with 'class' morality, which can be summarized as follows: Good is what at any given moment is required by authority. Naturally, such a morality, together with the propagation and stimulation of class and national animosities, has totally demoralized society and deprived it of any non-opportunistic moral criteria.

As an example, I might cite the unusual increase in casual thievery (as compared with a decrease in professional theft). Here is a typical case: Two young workers are on their way to visit friends. Walking along the street, they see an open ground-floor window. They slip in and grab some trifle or other. Had the window been shut, they would simply have passed on without more ado. One constantly sees people enter a house without a greeting, eat without removing their hats or swear coarsely in the presence of their small children. All this is normal behaviour and not in the least exceptional.

Thus the Christian ethic, which in Russia has a semi-pagan as well as official character, died out without being replaced by a Marxist ethic. (There is not space here to discuss it at length, but it is worth mentioning that Russia received her Christianity from Byzantium, which was rigid and moribund, and not from the developing and dynamic young Western civilization. This could not but deeply influence subsequent Russian history.) 'Marxist doctrine' was revised and reversed to suit current needs too often for it to become a viable ideology. And now as the regime becomes ever more bureaucratic, it becomes ever less ideological.

The need for an ideological underpinning forces the regime to look towards a new ideology, namely, Great Russian[34] nationalism, with its characteristic cult of strength and expansionist ambitions. Something similar took place at the beginning of the century, when the traditional monarchist ideology was replaced by a narrow nationalism. The Tsarist regime even introduced into everyday speech the expression 'genuinely Russian people' in distinction to the simpler term 'Russian', and inspired the creation of the Union of the Russian People.[35]

A regime grounded in such an ideology needs external and internal enemies who are not so much 'class' enemies (for instance, 'American imperialists' and 'anti-Soviet elements') as national enemies (for instance, Chinese and Jews). Such a nationalistic ideology, although it may prove temporarily useful to the regime, is very dangerous for a country in which those of Russian nationality constitute less than half the total population.

The need for a viable nationalist ideology is not only acutely felt by the regime, but nationalist feelings also appear to be taking hold in Soviet society, primarily in official literary and artistic circles (where they have evidently developed as a reaction to the considerable role of Jews in official Soviet art). Beyond these circles, these feelings have a centre of sorts in the 'Rodina' (Fatherland) Club.[36] The ideology can perhaps be called 'neo-Slavophile', although it should not be confused with the 'Christian ideology' – partially tinged with Slavophilism – which we discussed earlier. Its central features are an interest in Russianness, a belief in the messianic role of Russia and an extreme scorn and hostility towards everything non-Russian.

Since it was not inspired directly by the regime but arose spontaneously, the regime regards the new nationalism with a certain mistrust (an example of this is the ban on the film *Andrei Rubliov*),[37] yet at the same time with considerable tolerance. It could become a force to be reckoned with at any moment.

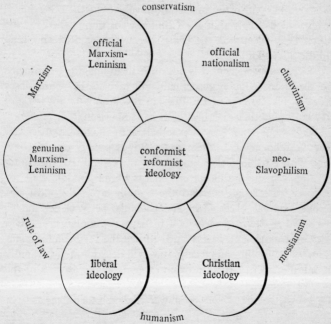

What I have said about the interrelationships of ideologies in contemporary Soviet society may be depicted graphically. The connecting lines in the above diagram show what links these ideologies; it is fairly clear what separates them. 'Reformist ideology', if its 'ideals' are to be taken in the exact sense of the word, should have been linked most closely with 'liberal ideology', but because of its extreme conformism and spirit of accommodation – which can be expressed in the words, 'Everything will get better later on; meanwhile we must live' – I have placed it in the centre of all the other ideologies.

What, then, are the beliefs and guiding ideas of this people with no religion or morality? They believe in their own national strength, which they demand that other peoples fear, and they are guided by a recognition of the strength of their own regime, of which they themselves are afraid. (It goes without saying that most Russians approved, or regarded with indifference, the Soviet military invasion of Czechoslovakia. On the other hand, they resented deeply that the Chinese went unpunished for the March 1969 clashes on the Ussuri River border between China and the Soviet Union.)

Under this assessment it is not difficult to imagine what forms and directions popular discontent will take if the regime loses its hold. The horrors of the Russian revolutions of 1905–7 and 1917–20 would then look like idylls in comparison.

There is, of course, a counterbalancing factor to these destructive tendencies. Contemporary Soviet society can be compared with a triple-decker sandwich – the top layer is the ruling bureaucracy; the middle layer consists of the 'middle class' or the 'class of specialists'; and the bottom layer, the most numerous, consists of the workers, peasants, petty clerks and so on. Whether Soviet society will manage to reorganize itself in a peaceful and painless way and survive the forthcoming cataclysm with a minimum of casualties will depend on how rapidly the middle layer of the sandwich expands at the expense of the other two and on how rapidly the 'middle class' and its organisation grow, whether faster or slower than the distintegration of the system.

It should be noted, however, that there is another powerful factor which works against the chance of any kind of peaceful reconstruction and which is equally negative for all levels of society: this is the extreme isolation in which the regime has placed both society and itself. This isolation has not only separated the regime from society, and all sectors of society from each other, but also put the country in extreme isolation from the rest of the world. This isolation has created for all – from the bureaucratic élite to the lowest social levels – an almost surrealistic picture of the world and of their place in it. Yet the longer this state of affairs helps to perpetuate the *status quo,* the more rapid and decisive will be its collapse when confrontation with reality becomes inevitable.

Summing up, it can be said that as the regime becomes progressively weaker and more self-destructive it is bound to clash – and there are already clear indications that this is happening – with two forces which are already undermining it: the constructive movement of the 'middle class' (rather weak) and the destructive movement of the 'lower classes', which will take the form of extremely damaging, violent and irresponsible action once its members realize their relative immunity from punishment. How long, though, will it be before the regime faces such an upheaval, and how long will it be able to bear the strain?

This question can be considered in two ways, depending on whether the regime itself takes decisive and forthright measures to rejuvenate itself or whether it merely continues to make the minimal necessary changes so as to stay in power, as it is doing now. To me, the second alternative appears more likely because it requires less effort, because it appears to be the less dangerous course and because it corresponds to the sweet illusions of today's 'Kremlin visionaries'.[38]

However, some mutations within the regime are also theoretically possible: for instance, a militarization of the regime and a transition to an openly nationalistic policy (this could be accomplished by a military *coup d'état* or by the gradual transfer of power into the hands of the military).

Such a policy would no longer disguise the regime's actions beneath the cloak of 'protecting the interests of the international Communist movement' in order to make some sort of gesture towards the independent and semi-independent Communist parties in the outside world. (As for the role of the army, it is constantly growing. This can be seen by anyone, for example, who compares today's ratio of military officers to civilians on the reviewing stand on top of Lenin's Mausoleum during parades with what it was ten or fifteen years ago.)

Another possible and very different mutation of the regime could occur through economic reforms and the relative liberalization of the system that would follow such reforms. (This could be achieved by increasing the role in the political leadership of pragmatic economists who understand the need for change.)

Neither of these possibilities appears unlikely on the face of it. However, the party machine, against which either *coup* would in effect be directed, is so closely intertwined with the military and economic establishments that both groups, if they pursued the aim of change, would very soon bog down in the same old quagmire. Any fundamental change would require such a drastic shake-up in personnel from top to bottom that, understandably, those who personify the regime would never embark on it. To save the regime at the cost of firing themselves would seem to them too exorbitant and unfair a price to pay.

On the question of how long the regime can survive, several interesting historical parallels may be cited. At present, at least some of the conditions that led to the first and second Russian revolutions probably exist again: a caste-ridden and immobile society, a rigid governmental system which openly clashes with the need for economic development, general bureaucratization and the existence of a privileged bureaucratic class, and national animosities within a multi-national state in which certain nations enjoy privileged status.

Under these same conditions, the Tsarist regime would probably have survived quite a while longer and would possibly have undergone some kind of peaceful modernization had the governing class not fantastically misjudged the general situation and its own strength, and pursued a policy of foreign expansion that overtaxed its powers. In fact, had the government of Nicholas II not gone to war against Japan, there would have been no revolution of 1905–7, and had it not gone to war against Germany, there would have been no revolution in 1917. (Strictly speaking, it did not start either of these wars itself, but it did its utmost to see that they were started.)

Why regimes that have become internally stagnant tend to develop a militantly ambitious foreign policy I find hard to say. Perhaps they seek a way out of their domestic problems through their foreign policies. Perhaps, on the other hand, the ease with which they can suppress internal opposition creates in their minds an illusion of omnipotence. Or perhaps it is because the need to have an external enemy, deriving from internal policy aims, builds up such momentum that it becomes impossible to halt the growth of hostility. This view is supported by the fact that every totalitarian regime decays without itself noticing it.

Why did Nicholas I need the Crimean War, which brought down the system he had created? Why did Nicholas II need the wars with Japan and Germany? The present regime, curiously enough, embodies traits of the reigns of both Nicholas I and Nicholas II, and, in its internal policy, probably that of Alexander III also. The best comparison, though, is with the Bonapartist regime of Napoleon III. In such a comparison the Middle east corresponds to the latter's Mexico, Czechoslovakia to the Papal States, and China to Imperial Germany.

II

The question of China needs to be considered in detail. Like our country, China has lived through a revolution and a civil war and, like ourselves, has made use of Marxist doctrine to consolidate the country. Also, as in our country, the further the revolution developed, the more Marxist doctrine became a camouflage which more or less concealed nationalist and imperialist aims.

To put it in general terms, our revolution has passed through three stages: (1) international; (2) national, linked with a colossal purge of the old cadres; and (3) military-imperialist, ending with the establishment of control over half of Europe. Then began the 'revolution at the top' – the transition from bloodstained Stalinist dynamism, first, to relative stability and then to the present-day stagnation.

It seems to me that the Chinese revolution is passing through the same stages: the international period has been followed by a nationalist period (borrowing from us even its terminology – for instance, the term 'cultural revolution', introduced by Stalin). In the logic of events a period of external expansionism must ensue.

My argument may be countered by the assertion that China does not want war and that, despite her very aggressive tone, her actions since the Communist victory in 1949 show her to be a peaceful and not an aggressive power. However, this is not the case.

First, the logic of her internal development has already brought China to the stage of external expansionism. Second, China has already demonstrated her aggressive tendencies towards countries where she did not expect to encounter strong resistance, for example, India. (I am not speaking here about the legality or illegality of China's territorial claims on other countries, particularly India, but only about the methods of their settlement.)

Nevertheless, the impression has been created that China wants to achieve her aims without herself taking part in a global war, but rather by pitting the Soviet Union and the United States against each other, in which case she could then come forward as the arbiter and supreme controller of the fate of the world. This China has failed to achieve, and the fact has long been realized by the Chinese leaders. Evidently this situation will lead, indeed already is leading, to a thorough reassessment of China's foreign policy.

Meanwhile, the relentless logic of revolution is propelling China towards a war which the Chinese leaders hope will solve the country's economic and social problems and secure for China a leading place in the modern world. (Her problems are primarily extreme overpopulation of some areas, hunger and an agriculture that needs extensive rather than intensive development and requires acquisition of new territories.)

Finally, in such a war China will be seeking national revenge for the centuries of humiliation and dependence forced on her by foreign powers. The main obstacle in the way to achieving these global goals is the existence of two superpowers, the Soviet Union and the United States, which, however, do not form a common front against China since they are themselves mutually antagonistic. Naturally, China takes this into account, and launches verbal onslaughts equally against 'American imperialism' and 'Soviet revisionism and social imperialism'. None the less, the real contradictions, and therefore the possibilities for a head-on conflict, are much greater between China and the Soviet Union than between China and the United States.

It may be assumed that the United States will not start a war with China, and China herself will simply be unable to wage such a war in the decades to come. Since she lacks a common border with the United States, she would be unable to exploit her superiority in numbers in a guerrilla war against the United States. Furthermore, she does not have a navy with which she could land troops on American territory. A nuclear-rocket duel – assuming that China succeeds in accumulating a sufficient nuclear arsenal in ten years – would result in mutual annihilation, which would not suit China's purpose at all. Moreover, China is interested in expanding her influence and territory primarily in Asia and not on the North American continent.

Whether the Chinese will manage to attain freedom of action in Asia as long as the United States maintains its might there is another matter. Evidently the United States will on every occasion attempt to stop China from expanding her influence southwards in any significant way, and this could lead to exhausting local wars, like that in Vietnam. But it is hardly thinkable that China would be interested in waging wars that will solve nothing, i.e. that would leave the United States itself unharmed.

Getting involved in such wars will seem even more risky to China so long as she has a treacherous foe to the north who would take advantage of any mistake she made. There is still another reason which may restrain China from expanding to the south or east: the overpopulation of these areas and the need either to feed or kill off their many millions of inhabitants.

The north is another matter. There lie the vast, sparsely populated territories of Siberia and the Soviet Far East which were once part of China's sphere of influence. These territories belong to the state that is China's main rival in Asia. It is essential for China somehow to eliminate or neutralize this rival if she is to play a dominant role in Asia and the world at large. Moreover, in comparison with the United States, the Soviet Union is a much more dangerous rival, which, as a totalitarian state with expansionist tendencies, may in one form or another strike the first blow.

China has already had a chance to appraise the methods of her 'ally-enemy' during the so-called period of 'eternal friendship' between the two countries. Then the Soviet Union, taking advantage of China's economic and military dependence, did all it could to subordinate China completely to its influence. When this failed, the Soviet Union cut off all economic aid and then tried to play on the nationalism of the smaller nations within China's borders.

Evidently Stalin, like Trotsky before him, understood that once the Communists were victorious in China the Soviet Union would in the long run acquire a dangerous enemy rather than an ally. Therefore he worked, on one hand, to spin out the struggle between the Communists and the Kuomintang, which was weakening China, and, on the other, to deepen the divisions within the Communist Party, and in particular to oppose the influence of Mao Tse-tung.

True, there was a time when the Chinese People's Republic and the Soviet Union may have given the impression of being allies, especially since they paid homage to one and the same ideology. However, the absolute antagonism of their national-imperial interests and the conflicting character of the internal processes in each country – 'proletarianization' and the rise of a fearsome 'revolutionary curve' in China and 'deproletarianization' and a cautious descent along the same curve in the Soviet Union – quickly put an end to any pretence of unity.

At first, China wanted to achieve her aims by 'peacefully absorbing' the Soviet Union and, after the victory of the revolution in 1949, offered to unite the two countries in a single Communist state. With a population three or four times as great as that of the Soviet Union, China would of course have secured for herself, gradually if not at once, a commanding position in such a state and, more importantly, would have immediately opened up Siberia, the Soviet Far East and Central Asia to her colonization.

Stalin did not accept this offer, and the Chinese postponed their plans for several decades; they will now have to carry them out by military means. Unlike in the above-mentioned case of the United States, China not only is capable of waging war against the Soviet Union but will also enjoy certain advantages in such a war.

Inasmuch as the Soviet Union is at present more powerful militarily than China, the Soviet regime, following a policy of imposing its will upon China while at the same time fearing her, will from time to time blackmail her – as the Tsarist regime did Japan at the beginning of the century – which will prompt the Chinese to start the war first and by the methods that will favour them most. However, China will not be able to start a war until she has accumulated considerable stockpiles – although they may still be smaller than those of the Soviet Union – of nuclear and conventional weapons.

The date for the outbreak of war will obviously depend on how soon China can achieve this goal. Taking five years as a minimum and ten years as a maximum, we may point to the period between 1975 and 1980 for the beginning of war between the Soviet Union and China. (Those who do not believe that, because of her economic backwardness, China can achieve rapid success in the field of nuclear rocketry should compare the forecasts of American and United Nations experts on how soon the Soviet Union would manufacture atomic and hydrogen bombs with the actual deadlines achieved.)

Having acquired a sizeable nuclear arsenal, China will, as I see it, nevertheless start the war by conventional or even guerrilla means, hoping to make use of her colossal superiority in numbers and her experience in guerrilla warfare. She will confront the Soviet Union with the alternative of either accepting the methods of warfare chosen by herself or striking a nuclear blow and receiving one in retaliation.

The Soviet Union will probably choose the former path, because to wage nuclear war, even with an anti-missile defence system, would be extremely dangerous, not to say suicidal. At the same time, the Soviet Union's superiority in conventional arms may give the Soviet leaders the impression that the Chinese Army can be destroyed or at least repelled by conventional means.

The actual moment of the outbreak of war may, in fact, be difficult to poinpoint: as her nuclear capability expands, China will increasingly provoke limited skirmishes along her 4,000-mile boundary with the Soviet Union, infiltrate small detachments into Soviet territory and spark off other sorts of local clashes. These skirmishes will be escalated into total war at the moment most suitable to China. It will thus prove very difficult for the Soviet Union to determine when to launch a nuclear attack against China.

Another logical possibility must also be considered: the Soviet leadership, considering China a potential nuclear rival and aggressor, may decide in favour of a preventive nuclear strike against China's nuclear centres before China has succeeded in amassing enough nuclear weapons to launch a powerful retaliatory blow. The leadership would be able to launch such a strike after fomenting border skirmishes and then presenting China to the Soviet people and world public opinion as the aggressor.

It seems unlikely that a bureaucratic regime would resort to such a desperate measure without also considering the position of the nuclear powers. But even if this measure is taken, it will not prevent a war; on the contrary, it will signal its beginning. After all, though China's main rocket bases would be destroyed, China would not. She would immediately retaliate by launching an exhausting guerrilla war that would be equally terrible for the

Soviet Union whether it was fought on Soviet or Chinese territory.

Strictly speaking, there is still another possibility to consider: an attempt to eliminate China's might by a conventional invasion and occupation of all or part of the country. However, in view of China's great superiority in numbers and her government's complete control over the country, such an invasion seems to me unlikely.

Will the Soviet regime, in the event of a Chinese guerrilla war, decide on the total destruction by nuclear weapons of all China's villages and towns and the whole Chinese population of 800 million people? It is difficult to imagine so apocalyptic a picture, but it is entirely conceivable since, as we know, it is precisely fear which drives people to take the most desperate actions. One can only hope that the other nuclear powers will not allow this to happen, since such an action would endanger the entire rest of the world.

It may be that China foresees the possibility of such a preventive strike. If that is so, she will follow a more cautious policy over the next five years and even flirt with the Soviet Union, something she has not done previously for reasons of internal politics. Diplomatic and possibly party contacts – though meaningless – would follow, ambiguous declarations would be made offering the prospect of reconciliation, and the tone of attacks on 'Soviet revisionism and social imperialism' would be slightly softened. At the same time, however, anti-Soviet propaganda within China would not let up, so that the Chinese people would be kept constantly on the alert for critical developments. At the same time, China might seek closer contacts with the United States, and then much would depend on those two countries' relations.

But first I believe that a preventive strike will not be made, and for at least two reasons: first, because of the extreme danger of such a strike if it is launched before all other means have been exhausted; and, second, because the possibility of Chinese aggression is not so self-evident as to warrant such risky action. Accordingly, China will accumulate a sufficient nuclear potential to be able to threaten the Soviet Union with reprisals should the latter contemplate using its nuclear advantage for purposes of self-defence. In this way, the Soviet Union will be forced into a guerrilla war of colossal territorial extent along both sides of a 4,000-mile frontier.

The possibility is not to be excluded that before attacking the Soviet Union China will test her strength against some small neutral country which was once in her sphere of influence and which has a Chinese minority. This would be a trial balloon for the forthcoming 'great proletarian revolutionary wars'.

Although, presumably, plans have long since been drawn up for the eventuality of a war with China, the Soviet Union, in my opinion, is not prepared, either technically or psychologically, for guerrilla or semi-guerrilla warfare. For the last two decades, our country has come to think of war as a clash between two armies equipped with the most modern resources, almost as a 'pushbutton war', a war in the West, against countries of Western culture and, finally, against numerically smaller land armies. All this has undoubtedly influenced military thinking in ways that will be very difficult to alter. Furthermore, the minds of the people are better prepared for war against 'the Americans' or 'the imperialists', for attacks from the air and for land war in Europe.

It is, of course, very difficult to foretell how the military action will develop, whether Soviet troops will succeed in bursting into China and occupying a considerable part of the country, or whether the Chinese, on the other hand, will slowly but steadily infiltrate into Soviet territory. In any case, the Soviet Union will be facing the same difficulties that its enemies have faced in the past.

In the first place, the actual methods of guerrilla warfare have, from the seventeenth century onwards, been the methods applied by the Russians against compact armies invading Russian territory. They have hardly ever been applied against Russian armies invading civilized Europe.

Second, from the very outset the Soviet armies will have to cope with enormously extended lines of communication, because the war will be fought along the Soviet Union's boundaries, thousands of miles from the principal economic and demographic centres.*

Third, the Russian soldier, while very often inferior to his adversary in culture, has usually surpassed him in toughness, endurance and an undemanding nature. But these advantages, so important in guerrilla warfare, will now be on the side of the Chinese. The Soviet press is already at work ridiculing the Chinese soldier as fanatical, yet puny and cowardly. Here, however, is the opinion of a Soviet military expert who worked for several years in China:

The Chinese soldier is superior to ours – hardy, not inclined to grumble and brave. He has immense mobility in the field. For a Chinese soldier to march seventy kilometres in a day is simply a trifle . . . Our infantrymen, who were quite amazed by the Chinese infantry, came to the conclusion that it is the best infantry in the world.†

Finally, since the arena will be the Far East, Siberia and Kazakhstan or adjacent regions on the Chinese side of the border, the war will be waged in areas which are sparsely populated or inhabited by non-Russians. These conditions will offer ample opportunity for guerrilla infiltration as well as serious difficulties in supplying large armies with sophisticated equipment and material.

All signs thus point to a war that will be protracted and exhausting, with no quick victory for either side. With this in mind, it is worth considering three problems: the attitude of the United States towards a Soviet-Chinese war; its consequences in Europe; and the resulting situation within the Soviet Union.

*The seriousness of that problem can be realized by recalling the difficulties the Germans faced during their advance into the Northern Caucasus in 1942, when they were forced to resort to camels to transport fuel for their tanks. At present European Russia is connected with the Far East by only one main railway line, which in many sections consists of only one track, though a second is under construction and several stages have been completed. An airlift extended over a long period would prove extremely costly and highly unreliable.

†V. M. Primakov, *Notes of a Volunteer* (Moscow, 1967), p. 212.

Since the Second World War the United States has appeared interested in an agreement and eventual partnership with the Soviet Union. The first step in this direction was made by President Roosevelt and led to the division of Germany and the whole of Europe and to a decade of 'cold war'. However, this did not discourage the Americans. Both in the Khrushchev era and today they continue to act on the assumption that it will be possible to reach an agreement with the Soviet Union in the not too distant future and together to solve the problems of the world.

This approach is obviously based not on any special sympathies for the Soviet system – although Americans hungrily and impatiently seize upon any insignificant development that can be interpreted as a sign of its 'liberalization' – but on the fact that in the present-day world the Soviet Union is the only real force that comes close to matching the power of the United States. It is probably this genuine parity which generates the desire for agreement and cooperation.

From this point of view, however, it is obvious that as China rises in power and influence, the United States will increasingly gravitate towards an agreement with her. American liberals will then begin to find in the regime of Mao Tse-tung or his successors as many attractive features as they saw in the regimes of Stalin or Khrushchev.

By pursuing a policy of encouraging Communism where the people do not want it and opposing it where they do want it, the United States has not only contributed to the division of Europe but also damaged its relations with China. It can be said that its national interests did not oblige the United States to do this. In its relations with China, the United States was guided by the policy of 'containing Communism', Communism being seen as an internationally coordinated phenomenon.

In so doing it helped to draw closer together the two Communist giants, the Soviet Union and China. At least ten years had to pass before the great differences between them came to the surface. Furthermore, the United States tied its own hands by supporting the regime of Chiang Kai-shek, which proved to be unviable (it was unable to hold out on the mainland of China and today it could not survive on Taiwan without American support; it is possible, however, that economically, thanks again to the United States, Taiwan is much more developed than mainland China).

If, on the other hand, the United States had supported Mao Tse-tung during the Civil War, this would have averted the rapprochement between China and the Soviet Union, avoided the Korean War and helped considerably in softening the Communist regime in China.

True, the United States is perhaps beginning gradually to abandon its former policy towards China, and it is difficult therefore to forecast its attitude towards the possible military confrontation between China and the Soviet Union. A great deal will depend also on China's relationship with the United States on the eve of war with the Soviet Union, as well as on the outcome of the Taiwan and Vietnam problems.

Thus, in analysing the problems of a United States rapprochement with either the Soviet Union or China on a broader historical plane, it should be noted that any such cooperation would have to be based not only on a balance of world forces and the desire on the part of each power to preserve its position in the world, but also on a community of national interests and aims.

I therefore believe that a rapprochement between the United States and the Soviet Union would make sense only after serious steps towards democracy were taken in the USSR. Until such time, any agreements on the part of the Soviet Union will be motivated either by fear of China or by an attempt to preserve the regime with the aid of American economic assistance (similar to the loans given by France to the Tsarist regime, which prolonged its existence by several years), or by the desire to use American friendship to install or maintain Soviet influence in other countries. In addition, of course, there is the interest of both countries in preserving their commanding roles in the world by mutual cooperation. This last objective is apparent, for example, in Soviet–American cooperation to prevent the proliferation of nuclear weapons.

Apart from a few benefits, such a 'friendship', based as it would be on hypocrisy and fear, would bring the United States nothing but the same sort of troubles that arose from the cooperation between Roosevelt and Stalin. Cooperation presupposes mutual reliance, but how can one rely on a country that has been capable of no other aim over the centuries than distending itself and sprawling in all directions like sour dough? A genuine rapprochement must be based on similarity of interests, culture and traditions, and on mutual understanding. Nothing like this exists.

What is there in common between a democratic country, with its idealism and pragmatism, and a country without beliefs, without traditions, without culture and without the ability to do an honest job? The popular ideology of our country has always been the cult of its own strength and vastness, and the basic theme of its cultured minority has been the description of its own weakness and alienation. Russian literature is a vivid example of this.

Russia's Slavic state has been created in turn by Scandinavians, Byzantines, Tatars, Germans and Jews. In each case the state has destroyed its creators. It has betrayed all its allies as soon as it found the slightest advantage in doing so. It has never taken seriously any of its agreements. And it has never had anything in common with anyone.

One can hear nowadays in Russia remarks like 'The United States will help us because we are white and the Chinese are yellow.' It will be very sad if the United States also adopts such a racist attitude. The world's only real hope for a better future lies not in a race war but in interracial cooperation. The best example of this could be good relations between China and the United States.

Undoubtedly, in the course of time China will raise the standard of living of her people considerably and will move into a period of liberalization. This, together with her traditional faith in spiritual values, will make her a remarkable partner for democratic America. In this, naturally, a great deal will depend on the United States itself, on whether it will continue to follow its rigid policy towards China or whether it will correct its previous mistakes and look for new approaches.

If the United States realizes all these possibilities, it will not help the Soviet Union in a war against China, especially since we know that China is incapable of totally destroying the Soviet Union. In such an event, the Soviet Union will face China by itself. And what will our European allies do?

After the Second World War the Soviet Union succeeded in creating along its western frontier a chain of neutral states, including Germany, and thus guaranteed its security in Europe. Such states, with 'interim' regimes like the one in Czechoslovakia until 1948, for instance, might have served as buffers between the West and the Soviet Union and guaranteed a stable situation in Europe. Their basic difference from the buffer states of the period between the world wars would have lain in the fact that they could have served not as a *cordon sanitaire* for the West against the Soviet Union, but as a connecting bridge with it.

However, the Soviet Union, by pursuing the Stalinist policy of territorial expansion and the deliberate fostering of international tension, extended its sphere of influence to the farthest possible limit and thereby created a danger for itself. Inasmuch as the existing situation in Europe is maintained only through the constant pressure of the Soviet Union, it may be assumed that as soon as this pressure lets up or disappears, considerable changes will occur in Central and Eastern Europe. This pressure, we may observe, is sometimes deliberately intensified as in the Berlin crisis, and sometimes it takes on a purely hysterical character.

Now as soon as it becomes clear that the military conflict between the Soviet Union and China will be protracted, that all the forces of the Soviet Union are being transferred to the East, and that the USSR cannot look after its interest in Europe, Germany will surely be reunited. It is entirely possible that West Germany, in order to hasten this process, will extend support in some form or another to China.

It is hard to predict whether reunification will come about through the absorption of East Germany by West Germany or whether the leaders of East Germany who will follow Walter

Ulbricht, understanding what is at stake, will agree to a voluntary merger with Bonn in order to preserve some of their privileges. Whatever the case, a reunited Germany with a fairly pronounced anti-Soviet orientation will create an entirely new situation in Europe.

Clearly, the reunification of Germany will coincide with a process of de-Sovietization in the East European countries and will considerably hasten this process. Paradoxical as it may seem, the Soviet Union can already rely more on President Nixon, the leader of 'American imperialism', than on such allies as Ceausescu of Romania or Dr Husak of Czechoslovakia. The situation in Eastern Europe today somewhat resembles the situation after the revolutions of 1848, when the democratization that was hoped for did not come about and yet the old regime was shaken.

It is difficult to say how the de-Sovietization of Eastern Europe will proceed and whether it will assume the 'Hungarian', the 'Romanian' or the 'Czechoslovak' form. However, it will surely result in national-Communist regimes, which in each country will somewhat resemble their pre-Communist regimes – liberal democracy in Czechoslovakia, a military-nationalist regime in Poland and so forth. Meanwhile, several countries at least, such as Hungary and Romania, will promptly follow their pro-German orientation.

The Soviet Union could evidently prevent all this only by a military occupation of all Eastern Europe aimed at creating a safe rear area for its Far Eastern front. In fact, however, such a rear area would become a second front, that is, a front against the Germans, who would receive the help of the peoples of Eastern Europe – something the Soviet Union could not afford.

It is more likely, therefore, that the de-Sovietized countries of Eastern Europe will dash around like horses without their bridles and, finding the Soviet Union powerless in Europe, will present territorial claims that have long been hushed up but not forgotten: Poland to Lvov and Vilna, Germany to Kaliningrad (Königsberg), Hungary to Transcarpathia, Romania to Bessarabia. The possibility that Finland will lay claim to Viborg and Pechenga is also not to be excluded. It is probable, as well, that as the Soviet Union becomes more deeply involved in the war, Japan, too, will present territorial claims, first to the Kurile Islands, then to Sakhalin and later, depending on China's success, even to a portion of the Soviet Far East.

Apparently the leaders of the Soviet regime are aware of the threat from Germany and Japan that would arise in the course of a conflict with China, and they might be inclined to take drastic steps towards a rapprochement with those countries. Yet because of the bureaucratic nature of the regime, Moscow cannot be expected to take any decisive steps in this direction.

Briefly, then, the Soviet Union will have to pay up in full for the territorial annexations of Stalin and for the isolation in which the neo-Stalinists have placed the country. However, the events most important to the future of the Soviet Union will occur within the country itself.

Naturally, the beginning of a war against China, which will be portrayed as the aggressor, will cause a flare-up of Russian nationalism – 'We'll show them!' – simultaneously raising the hopes of the non-Russian nationalities within the Soviet Union. As the war progresses, Russian nationalism will decline while non-Russian nationalism will rise. Indeed, the war will go on for some time without having any direct effect on the emotional perceptions of the people or their way of life, as was the case during the last war with Germany, but all the while exacting a mounting toll of lives.

Eventually the conflict will give rise to a steadily deepening moral weariness with a war waged far away and for no apparent reason. Meanwhile, economic hardships, particularly related to food supplies, will appear, which will be felt all the more deeply because of the recent slow but steady rise in the standard of living.

Since the regime is not lenient enough to permit any legal channels for the expression of discontent and thus its alleviation, and since at the same time it is not brutal enough to rule out all possibility of protest, there will ensue sporadic eruptions of popular dissatisfaction, or local riots, caused, for instance, by shortages of bread. These will be put down with the help of troops, which, in turn, will accelerate the collapse of the army. Naturally, the so-called internal security troops will be used – and, if possible, troops of a nationality other than that of the population that is rioting, but this will merely sharpen enmities among the nationalities.

As the regime's difficulties mount and as it appears ever more incapable of coping with its tasks, the 'middle class' will grow increasingly hostile. The defection of allies and the territorial claims advanced in both West and East will increase the feelings of isolation and hopelessness. Extremist organizations, which will have made an appearance by this time, will begin to play an ever greater role. Simultaneously, the nationalist tendencies of the non-Russian peoples of the Soviet Union will intensify sharply, first in the Baltic area, the Caucasus and the Ukraine, then in Central Asia and along the Volga.

In many cases, party officials among the various nationalities may become the proponents of such tendencies, and their reasoning will be: 'Let Russian Ivan solve his own problems.' They will aim for national separateness for still another reason: if they can fend off the growing general chaos, they will be able to preserve their own privileged positions.

Meanwhile, the bureaucratic regime, which, with its customary half-measures, will be incapable of simultaneously pursuing the war, solving the economic problems and suppressing or satisfying popular demands, will retreat further and further into itself, losing control over the country and even contact with reality.

A major defeat at the front, or a serious eruption of popular discontent in the capital, such as strikes or an armed clash, will be enough to topple the regime. Naturally, if by this time complete power has passed into the hands of the military, the regime, thus modified, will hang on a little longer. But if it fails to solve the most urgent problems, which in time of war are almost insoluble, it will then fall in an even more terrible manner. If I have determined the time of the outbreak of war with China correctly, the collapse of the regime will occur sometime between 1980 and 1985.

Obviously, the Democratic Movement, which the regime through constant repression has prevented from gathering strength, will be in no condition to take control into its own hands – in any event, not long enough to solve the problems of the country. The unavoidable 'de-imperialization' will take place in an extremely painful way. Power will pass into the hands of extremist elements and groups, and the country will begin to disintegrate into anarchy, violence and intense national hatred.

The boundaries of the new states which will then begin to emerge in the territory of the former Soviet Union will be extremely hard to determine. The resulting military clashes will be exploited by the neighbours of the Soviet Union – above all, of course, by China.

But it is also possible that the 'middle class' will prove strong enough to keep control in its own hands. In that case, the granting of independence to the various Soviet nationalities will come about peacefully and some sort of federation will be created, similar to the British Commonwealth or the European Economic Community. Peace will be concluded with China, which will also have been weakened by the war, and the conflicts with European neighbours will be settled on mutually acceptable terms. It is even possible that the Ukraine, the Baltic Republics and European Russia will enter a Pan-European federation as independent units.

A third possibility also exists – namely, that none of these things may happen.

But what will, in fact, happen? I have no doubt that this great Eastern Slav empire, created by Germans, Byzantines and Mongols, has entered the last decades of its existence. Just as the adoption of Christianity postponed the fall of the Roman Empire but did not prevent its inevitable end, so Marxist doctrine has delayed the break-up of the Russian Empire – the third Rome – but it does not possess the power to prevent it.

Carrying this analogy further, one can also assume that in Central Asia, for instance, there could survive for a long time a state that considered itself the successor of the Soviet Union – a state which combined traditional Communist ideology, phraseology and ritual with the traits of Oriental despotism – a kind of contemporary Byzantine Empire.

But although the Russian Empire has always sought maximum isolation from the world, it would hardly be correct to discuss its fall in a context unrelated to the rest of the world.

Scientific progress is generally considered the fundamental direction of contemporary development, and total nuclear war is regarded as the basic threat to civilization. And yet even scientific progress, with every passing year consuming progressively more of the world's production, could become regressive and civilization may perish without benefit of a dazzling nuclear explosion.

Although scientific and technical progress changes the world before our very eyes, it is, in fact, based on a very narrow social foundation. The more significant scientific successes become, the sharper will be the contrast between those who achieve and exploit them and the rest of the world. Soviet rockets have reached Venus, while in the village where I live potatoes are still dug by hand. This should not be regarded as a comical comparison; it is a gap which may deepen into an abyss.

The crux of the matter is not the way in which potatoes are dug but the fact that the level of thinking of most people is no higher than this manual level of potato-digging. In fact, although in the economically developed countries science demands more and more physical and human resources, the fundamental principles of modern science are understood by only an insignificant minority. For the time being this minority, in collusion with the ruling elite, enjoys a privileged status. But how long will this continue?

Mao Tse-tung talks about the encircling of the 'city' – meaning the economically developed countries – by the 'village' – meaning the underdeveloped countries. In fact, the economically developed countries constitute only a small part of the total world population. But what is more, even in the developed countries the 'city' is encircled by the 'village' – the village in the literal sense of the word or former village dwellers who have only recently moved to the city. And even in the cities the people who direct modern civilization and benefit from it are an insignificant minority.

Finally, in our inner world, too, the 'city' is encircled by the 'village' – the 'village' of the subconscious – and at the first disruption of our customary values we immediately feel it. Is not, in fact, this gap between city and village the greatest potential threat to our civilization?

The threat to the 'city' from the 'village' is all the greater in view of the fact that in the 'city' there exists a noticeable tendency towards the ever greater isolation of the individual, while the 'village' is aspiring to organization and unity. This gladdens the heart of Mao Tse-tung, but the inhabitants of the world's cities have reason, as I see it, to worry about their future.

Meanwhile, we are told, Western prognosticators are indeed worried by the growth of the cities and the difficulties brought on by the rapid pace of scientific and technological progress. Evidently, if 'futurology' had existed in Imperial Rome, where, as we are told, people were already erecting six-storey buildings and children's merry-go-rounds were driven by steam, the fifth-century 'futurologists' would have predicted for the following century the construction of twenty-storey buildings and the industrial utilization of steam power.

As we now know, however, in the sixth century goats were grazing in the Forum – just as they are doing now, beneath my window, in this village.

April–June 1969
Moscow and the village of Akulovo

An Open Letter to Kuznetsov

Anatoly Kuznetsov, a well-known and widely published Soviet writer, defected to the West in 1969 and now lives in London. Shortly after his defection, Kuznetsov made various public statements attempting to explain the situation of the Soviet writer and his own personal dilemma as a writer in Russia. One of these was an article, 'The Russian Writer and the KGB', which appeared in the Sunday Telegraph *on 10 August 1969. In November 1969 Amalrik wrote a reply to Kuznetsov, which was published in* Survey, *No. 74/75, and appears here by permission of the editor.*

Dear Anatoly Vasilevich,

I wanted to write to you as soon as I heard over the radio your appeal to people in general – and also to me – and your article 'The Russian Writer and the KGB'. I did not do this at once because I was living in the countryside from where my letter would scarcely reach you. But perhaps it has turned out for the best that I am writing to you several months later. First, I have heard of (I have not yet read) your other letters to the Pen Club and to Mr Miller and have been able to understand you better.

Second, it might have appeared that my voice – a voice which comes to you from the country which you have forsaken – would have sounded forth at the same time as the voices of those people in the West who condemned you for your flight and the method you chose for it.

This is not altogether so. I believe that if you as a writer were unable to work here or to publish your books in the form in which you wrote them, then it was not only your right but in a certain sense also your duty as a writer to leave this place. And if you were not able just to pack up and go as anybody in the West can do, then the persistence and cunning which you displayed to this end merits only respect. The fact that you used the methods of your persecutors and twisted them in this way round your little finger is in no way, I think, reprehensible, but the fact that you by your non-return and by means of a frank article turn an ominous report into an inoffensive, amusing piece of work does nothing but harm to the art of reports which exists only in our country.

However, in all that you have written and said while you have been abroad – at any rate as far as I have heard – there are two things that seem to me incorrect and which I therefore want to object to with all frankness.

You speak all the time of freedom, but of external freedom, the freedom around us, and you say nothing of the inner freedom, that is, the freedom according to which the authorities can do much to a man but by which they are powerless to deprive him of his moral values.

But, seemingly, such freedom and the responsibility attributed to it is a necessary prerequisite of external freedom. Perhaps in certain countries the freedom to express his thoughts is as freely available to a man as the air he breathes. But where this does not exist, such freedom, I think, can only come about as the result of a stubborn upholding of his inner freedom.

You say that the KGB has persecuted and blackmailed the Russian writer. Of course, what the KGB has done can only be condemned. But one does not understand what the Russian writer has done to oppose this. To struggle against the KGB is terrible, but what in effect threatened a Russian writer if before his first visit abroad he had refused to collaborate with the KGB? The writer would not have gone abroad – which he probably wanted to do very much – but he would have remained an honest man. In refusing in general to collaborate in this way he would have lost a portion, perhaps a considerable portion, of his external freedom but would have achieved a greater inner freedom. You keep saying they summoned me, they ordered me, the censorship always forced me on my knees, etc. It seems to me that if you had continually made concessions and done what you condemned in your heart you would not have deserved better treatment at the hands of the KGB or the censorship.

I think that I have a right to reproach you for this. I have always tried not to do that which I would condemn in my heart. I not only did not enter the Party as you did, but neither did I join the Komsomol, nor even the Pioneers – although as a small boy I was repeatedly urged to do this. I preferred to be expelled from university and to give up my hope of becoming a historian rather than to correct anything in my work which I myself considered correct. I preferred in general not to send my verses and plays to Soviet publishing houses rather than to mutilate them in the hope that they would be printed.

It would take a long time to relate how the KGB paid attention to me and so I will merely touch on the point you write about. In 1961 I was courteously invited by the KGB to write a general account of the mood of the intelligentsia and I equally courteously refused, upon which the matter ended.

In 1963 I was taken by night to the Lubyanka[1] and ordered to write a report against an American diplomat to the effect that he had subjected me and other Soviet citizens to malicious ideological brainwashing. I again refused, although on this occasion they had threatened me with criminal proceedings. In 1965 I refused outright to talk with them, which cost me an exile in Siberia. But the main thing is that, by living in this country and by continuing to write and do what I consider right, I can at any moment be sent to prison again or be dealt with in any other fashion. That is why I think I have the personal right to reproach you.

But perhaps I have no right to do this. Above all, because I am almost ten years younger than you and I was only lightly touched by that most terrible period which coincided with your youth and in which you were formed as an individual. Even now the regime exists, perhaps not only, but mainly, on the interest from the capital of fear amassed in those times. And it is a matter not only of the KGB but the fact that the whole atmosphere of Soviet life and of Soviet education is such that a man is already conditioned to meet with the KGB and to enter into the same relations with it as you did.

Perhaps there is one other reason why I have no right to reproach you, and that is that it can be objected against me that although you repeatedly compromised and even went as far as dishonourable submission, you thereby achieved – albeit in mutilated form – the publication of your books, received recognition as a writer in your own country and thereby made a contribution to its culture, whereas my plays, be they good or bad, belong only to me or to a narrow circle of people; neither in the eyes of the authorities nor in the eyes of society am I a writer and therefore whatever I say or write is of no importance to anybody; that my 'literary honesty' is, in the final analysis, of no more consequence for me than the virginity of a forty-year-old woman.

Again, you may answer my reproach by saying that much in life happens by chance, that it is not only that I have proudly rejected any opportunity of success in the conditions of this regime but that I have been rejected in certain circumstances, that if matters had turned out differently and I had been allowed to publish my article or play after certain changes had been made, would I have stood out against this offer – and having once taken the path of compromise how far would I have gone along it? And would I have written and done things in my life of which I would now be ashamed? This is also true.

Finally, ought one in general to reproach a man who has declared so emphatically that he has broken with his past and has not been afraid to speak of things which many people carry with them to the grave and has thereby shown, albeit partially, how the shameful mechanism of oppression works in our country?

Nevertheless, I do reproach you. Not because I want to criticize you personally, but because I want to criticize the philosophy of impotence and self-justification which runs through all you have said and written in the West. 'I was given no other choice,' you seem to be saying, and this sounds like a justification not only for yourself but for the whole of the Soviet creative intelligentsia – or at least for that 'liberal' part of it to which you belong.

67

You condemn, directly or indirectly, certain of its representatives, but inasmuch as you do not direct one word of condemnation to yourself, blaming the authorities for everything, I do not understand how you can make any demands on the rest. You want to say that you are all victims of oppression, but it seems to me that no oppression can be effective without those who are prepared to submit to it. I sometimes think that the Soviet 'creative intelligentsia' – that is, people accustomed to thinking one thing, saying another and doing a third – is as a whole an even more unpleasant phenomenon than the regime which gave it birth. Hypocrisy and the acceptance of things as they are foisted on it has become so much a part of it that it considers any attempt to act honourably as either a crafty provocation or madness. I have met people – and you have probably met more – who while secretly hating the authorities do everything they are ordered and, what is more, in doing so they hate the authorities even more. But they have an even stronger hatred for those who, in the words of your letter to Mr Miller, 'struggle noisily against' the authorities.

This is because the enraged authorities, making no distinction, may lash out not only at those who 'struggle noisily' but also at those who 'hate secretly'.

I do not mean that all those who desire greater freedom for themselves and their country should go to Red Square with banners. However, they ought to reject the customary cynicism which equates truth and lies, to believe in some moral values even if they are absurd and to try to acquire inner freedom. How this is to be done must obviously be decided by each person himself. Not everyone can come out openly against those conditions in which we live and maybe this is not always the best method. But it is always better to be silent than to utter falsehoods, better to refuse to publish any of your books than to put out something which is completely contrary to what one had written in the beginning, better to refuse a trip abroad than to become an informer through it or to 'report' by means of a false poem, better to refuse a press conference than to declare publicly that creative freedom exists in our country. If an individual person or the whole country actively want to be free they must achieve freedom somehow even if it be by means of non-cooperation with their oppressors. But sometimes to obtain this one must risk even the freedom one has – which, as I understand it, you were afraid to do.

The question which was often put to you in the West, namely, why do the people in the USSR not change the government if it is so bad, seemed to you naïve. This question seems completely reasonable to me. I would reply to it in this way: it is not that the people do not change the government because the government is good but because we ourselves are bad. We are passive, ignorant and fearful; we deceive ourselves with primitive myths and tangle ourselves with bureaucratic ways; we permit our most active citizens to be destroyed; the majority of us do not understand our situation; our intelligentsia is venal, frightened and deprived of moral criteria. Gradually, however, we are beginning to find ourselves strength – and this means that sooner or later much can change. But you do not talk in this fashion. Willy-nilly, you are trying to create the impression that all struggle is useless and that those who 'struggle noisily' are also hypocrites to a greater or lesser degree when they declare themselves to be 'for the Soviet regime', and as being opposed only to its particular or general short-comings as do Siniavsky or Solzhenitsyn.

Nonetheless, it is Siniavsky who is in prison and it is Solzhenitsyn who is 'persecuted and tormented'. But you, being totally against this regime and therefore a 'true opposition', remained silent and did what you were told by the authorities.

I think that all this is false. The word 'Soviet' by itself is scarcely a good defence against the regime. Perhaps the regime sees the greatest danger in those people who say that they are 'for the Soviet regime' but who understand by 'Soviet regime' not at all what the regime would wish. Not being personally acquainted with either Siniavsky or Solzhenitsyn I cannot judge how far their public position is sincere. It seems to me, however, that it deserves only respect in every case, as does the position of Daniel and many others. As for their books – and I consider

Solzhenitsyn the most significant contemporary Russian writer –
I suggest that they are not Soviet and not anti-Soviet, but simply
literature which wishes to be free.

Judging only by his books, it is impossible to say that Solzhenitsyn is 'persecuted and tormented' – he gives the impression
of a man capable of standing out against persecution, he has
already once preserved his inner freedom in prison and will evidently do so again if he is once more put in jail. From this we can
all derive strength.

And when you say that you wish to write freely and that it was
for this that you fled to the West I understand you and I react
with respect to the pragmatic coolheadedness with which you
managed to do this, but when you try to prove that your 'secret
hatred' and open collaboration here constituted 'true opposition',
hinting thereby that the opposition of Siniavsky or Solzhenitsyn
is false, and at the same time put yourself forward in the West as
the herald of this opposition, then I believe that you place yourself in a false position.

The KGB would scarcely be able, as you put it, to destroy
samizdat in two days and play a cat-and-mouse game with it.
Perhaps the KGB could arrest dozens of *samizdat* distributors
in a matter of two hours – and the fact that the KGB does not do
this proves, it seems to me, not its playfulness (although a game is
being played) but the uncertainty in which the KGB and the
regime as a whole find themselves. Apart from this, *samizdat* is
distributed not among individuals as you say but among thousands.

It seems to me that the pitiful role in which the KGB has
placed you and many of your colleagues has forced you subconsciously to overestimate its power. You write that we are
living in an Orwellian world, but if this is so you have contributed your mite to this world by your submissiveness and mys-
tical attitude towards the KGB.

But, however that may be, you have now entered another
world and have brought your 'secret hatred' to a place where it
can become open, but, alas, it will provoke neither an answering
hatred nor feelings of warm sympathy – rather a sympathetic

curiosity, but sometimes, as you have already been convinced, even a hostile curiosity.

It is in connection with this that I want to address to you my second reproach.

The impression is created that many people in the West have a very poor idea of the actual situation in our country and in particular of the situation of writers. Possibly this is because for people brought up since childhood in a different culture and with different social principles it is as hard to understand another world as it is to speak immediately in another language. Another reason is that information about many facets of our life does not in general reach the West or reaches it in very small quantities. In addition, those people whose obligation it is to supply the West with information consciously or unconsciously distort it. Therefore, it is not only the right but also the duty of every Russian who desires that Western public opinion should better understand his country and even by its authority help to achieve greater freedom for it, honestly to inform independent public opinion of what is happening in our country. To inform, but not to seek sympathy and even more not to try to provoke pity as you seem to me to be doing.

I think that your complaints move nobody, just as nobody is moved by my complaints or by those of anybody else, inasmuch as everyone has the strength to bear the misfortunes of others. I believe that the more calmly and objectively we illuminate the situation of the writer in our country and the less dramatically we point out to so-called 'progressive Western public opinion' its dishonesty towards us, the quicker we will be able to destroy the false reputation which the existing regime in our country has been able to create for itself abroad.

I speak of dishonesty because it is dishonest, when one enjoys complete freedom of speech and other freedoms in one's country or is obtaining for oneself greater freedoms and greater influence, to collaborate in any way with a regime which deprives its citizens of these freedoms and of any influence, to seek this or that justification for this regime or to enter into any contacts or dialogues with it.

I think that we have no right to condemn these people because their own problems cause them greater anxiety than all our sufferings, still less have we the right to demand that they crawl into our skins and themselves experience what we have to do. But also we ought not to complain to them, to seek their sympathy or to be offended if we do not find it. We must only speak the truth to them and to anyone who will listen, about the situation in our country. For it is our country itself which needs this in the first instance.

And I think we are still within our rights to say to them: if not only freedom for us but the principle of freedom in general is dear to you, think a little before you travel for the purposes of 'intellectual dialogue' to a country where the very concept of freedom has been distorted and think ten times before, in admiration of the Potemkin villages, you write reports on Russia which are full of a false significance.

In your desire to convince Western public opinion that the situation of the writers and of the whole people in our country is very grim you repeat several times that we have an allegedly fascist regime. But the point is not whether this is true or not but that until fascism was overthrown and exposed there were many people in the democratic countries who admired fascism or at any rate found in it certain merits. Perhaps they believed that fascism was not suitable for themselves but that it was perfectly all right for the Germans and Italians. Many people also hoped that if it were gradually drawn into the respectable society of various international organizations fascism would give up its bad ways. So that I do not know that your analogies achieve their aim.

I also do not know whether you acted correctly when you asked Mr Miller as President of the Pen Club to occupy himself with the fate of writers in Russia. Mr Miller, irrespective of what sort of writer or person he is, in his position has been compelled to occupy himself not with literature and its fate but with the politics surrounding literature – so it seems looking at the situation from Russia – and in the sphere of these politics has made it his task to bring the Soviet writers' organization into the Pen

Club. From the point of view of politics this would possibly constitute a great victory for Mr Miller, but what would it give from the point of view of literature? What gain would there be to our country if Kochetov or Yevtushenko were to go to Menton and state that creative freedom exists in the USSR? Is the position of the East German writers better than the position of Soviet writers because East Germany is a member of the Pen Club? In my opinion politics and art are incompatible and even opposed and therefore any politics which are carried out around art not only always harm the interests of art for the sake of purely political motives but also introduce into it a spirit of compromise which is foreign to art.

This is in general what I wanted to say to you. And one more thing: do not take to heart all that you hear in the West. The reproach has been made against you that as a result of your non-return the situation in our country will become even worse, that many of your colleagues will not be able to travel to the West. I do not think that the situation has become worse. The harm lies not in the fact that a routine pseudo-liberal piece of verse will not be published or that its author will not be allowed to travel abroad, but in the fact that many talented poets and prose writers have been deprived of the opportunity of becoming known: some are in general ceasing to write and others are embarking on the path of pitiful conformism. Here, your non-return will change nothing for good or ill. If you can explain this in the West it will be most important.

This is all right, providing you can convince the West that your relations with the KGB were the rule rather than the exception for the Soviet literary milieu. You hint, for example, that several well-known poets were, like yourself, informers. It seems to me, however, that the important thing is not that writers serve the KGB but that literature, like the KGB, fulfils a service function: the important thing is not whether your hints are justified or not but that all this poetic–political deception which flourished in Khrushchev's time and has proved to be not particularly needed by his successors bears as little relation to independent art as the writings of Kochetov. It even appears to me that Kochetov's sincere obscurantism deserves greater respect than the false rebelliousness of those who, together with vodka and caviare, were for a long time an export necessary to the regime.

I am writing to you in answer to articles and letters published openly by you and I therefore consider my letter to be open. Since I wish to have it published I wanted to write as briefly as possible but it has turned out unusually lengthy: either I cannot write or I wanted to touch upon too many things all at once. None the less, I am sending you this letter through the *Daily Telegraph* and I should be very glad if this respected newspaper will publish it. I would wish this above all so that people in the West should know that there is in our country another point of view with regard to your non-return than that which has been expressed in the Soviet press by your former colleagues.

Anatoly Vasilevich, I warmly and sincerely congratulate you on being now in a free country and I hope that this will be a big step for you on your path to inner freedom. Therefore I wish above all for you that your books which are written and published in conditions of freedom will turn out better and more interesting than those which were published under your name in the USSR.

Respectfully,
Andrei Amalrik
1 November 1969

I Want to be Understood Correctly

This letter, written in January 1970, appeared in Survey, *No. 74/75, and is reproduced by permission of the editor. Brief extracts also appeared in the* Daily Telegraph *on 23 February 1970 and the* Guardian *on 24 February 1970.*

Several decades of terror gave rise in my country not only to an atmosphere of fear but an attendant atmosphere of universal distrust and suspiciousness. Consequently when people appeared who dared to do what no one had dared to do earlier, or what was punished by immediate arrest, there were rumours about nearly all of them that if they were acting so boldly it must be by the permission or on the instructions of the secret police. These rumours originated with those who, from congenital or inculcated cowardice, would never themselves dare to do anything displeasing to the regime and could not understand that there might simply be people more courageous or desperate than themselves.

When, therefore, similar rumours about myself reached me I always felt upset but realized that they were inevitable. Also I was well aware that none of my friends or people to whom I am well known would take such a rumour seriously for a second and that none of my ill-wishers would dare to make such a statement publicly knowing they had not a single fact to support it. This is the situation in my own country.

Unfortunately I have discovered that there are also people in the West who follow the logic that 'if someone behaves unlike every one else, then there must be something fishy'. Moreover they permit themselves to give wide publicity to their inventions, while admitting that they have 'no answers, only suspicions'. It seems to me that if one has 'only suspicions' one should not in general publicly blacken someone – these 'suspicions', after all, are not merely of academic interest, they concern human honour and dignity.

However, since several American newspapers have already published a story that I might be a KGB agent, I would like to make public what I myself think about this.

As I understand this story was first put out by Mr Bradsher in the *Washington Evening Star* of 26 November 1969. When I first heard about this article I intended to write a short letter to the editor of the newspaper in order to refute the 'suspicions' contained in the article. I assumed that it was written in a manner which, although unpleasant for me, was nevertheless measured and restrained. When I finally succeeded in getting hold of the article and rereading it I found that it was nothing but a bucket of slops poured on my head. I do not wish therefore to write to the paper which printed such an article but will give it to American correspondents in Moscow and will be grateful to any American paper which will publish it.

Although Mr Bradsher begins his article in a semi-inquiring tone, it leaves the impression that he is not so much trying to investigate the question of who I am, as deliberately to blacken me. He distorts and juggles with facts, makes unpleasant allusions and reveals a typical police mentality incapable of looking at anything simply and feels himself obliged to seek something hidden and dishonourable underneath. At the same time he is determined not to make any assertion on his own personal responsibility, but refers all the time to certain 'specialists', 'a defector from the USSR', a 'man who knew Amalrik well a few years ago' – all of whom remain anonymous. This sort of article could well appear in *Pravda* with the sole difference that I would be called an agent of the CIA instead of the KGB.

Nevertheless, not being in a position to sue Mr Bradsher for defamation but wishing to defend myself, I will reply to his arguments in detail.

The first argument is my open letter to the Soviet novelist

Anatoli V. Kuznetsov, who recently defected to Britain and denounced secret police control of Soviet writers.

'This letter', continues Mr Bradsher, 'seemed to analysts here intended to destroy Kuznetsov's role in the West as a valiant defender of writers' freedom, and thereby to destroy his usefulness in anti-communist propaganda.' He adds that I 'rebuked him for his own admissions of serving the KGB as an informer'.

In my letter I criticize Kuznetsov by no means for revealing 'secret police control of Soviet writers'. In my eyes Kuznetsov's only courageous act was that he honestly spoke about his cooperation with the KGB and so partially revealed the mechanism for controlling writers. This is what I say in my letter.

Nor do I criticize Kuznetsov for fleeing abroad as some inattentive readers of my letter have supposed. On the contrary, I wrote that if he could not work freely in the USSR, it was not only his right but his duty as a writer to escape to a place where he could write what he wanted and publish what he wanted.

I criticize Kuznetsov for the fact that having got abroad he tries to fully justify his activity as an informer and his conformism in the USSR, attributing everything to the cruelty of the regime, and he justified the cowardly and passive behaviour of the majority of the Soviet intelligentsia which wants to be 'pitied' because it is not free but is not willing to make the slightest effort to seek that freedom. Thus I wrote that if we want to change the regime in our country, we must all take a share of personal responsibility for this.

I hope that Anatoli Vasilevich Kuznetsov has correctly understood the sense of my rebukes which I made not to 'compromise his role in the eyes of the West', but to show him that the independent people of his country neither take the same attitude towards him as the official Soviet press, nor that of those who value him from the point of view of his usefulness to 'anti-communist propaganda'.

It is hard for me to judge whether my letter 'destroys' this 'usefulness' or not, but I should like to say that for me 'propaganda' is the most revolting word, and that when I wrote my letter I was not thinking of communist or anti-communist propaganda but of the dignity of the Russian writer.

Mr Bradsher completely misrepresents my letter. I wrote that judging by his books Solzhenitsyn does not give the impression of a 'persecuted and tormented' man, that he is capable of withstanding any persecution, that he has already retained his inner freedom and dignity in prison once and will, I am sure, retain them again if he is once more put behind bars, and I add that we can all draw strength from Solzhenitsyn's example.

But Mr Bradsher presents this part of my letter thus:

'Amalrik said, "it is impossible to say that Solzhenitsyn . . . is persecuted and tormented" and added coolly that he could survive a further term of imprisonment.'

Mr Bradsher distorts my letter to Kuznetsov several more times. He writes: 'Amalrik claimed he preferred to remain silent and suffer than to lie for privileges,' and concludes that, since I am silent and at the same time 'apparently do not suffer' nevertheless, this raises a big question. In fact all I said in the letter is that it is better for people who cannot openly protest against the regime simply to keep quiet, rather than write and say the opposite to their own views.

The second argument is my return from Siberia, where I was exiled by the KGB, before my sentence was up. 'In 1966 the Russian Supreme Court revoked the sentence,' writes Mr Bradsher, 'and Amalrik returned to Moscow. A revocation was unusual, being allowed to return to Moscow even more unusual.' And he goes on: 'Perhaps he bought his way out of Siberian exile by agreeing to cooperate.'

Here again Mr Bradsher distorts the facts or simply does not know them.

The review of sentences is the most ordinary practice, connected not with agreements behind the scenes but with the simple fact that many cases are dealt with extremely incompetently by the lowest organs, and sentences are imposed manifestly without cause, and this forces the higher organs to change them somewhat, even if such cases have been 'cooked up' by the KGB. As for those who were convicted under the decree of 4 May 1961[1] like me, I do not know of a single case in which a person convicted for political reasons has served his full sentence under this decree, so crudely and unlawfully were these cases dealt with. The poet Joseph Brodsky's sentence was reviewed, like mine, and he was able to return to his native Leningrad ahead of time.[2] Much has been written about his case in the West and his poems have been published there. The poet Batshev (from the SMOG[3] group) and the artist Nedbailo also returned to Moscow from exile before their sentences were up. According to Mr Bradsher's logic, one should declare all of them agents of the KGB.

Even more absurd is his assertion that 'permission to return to Moscow is unusual'. Such permission is withheld only in cases where a person is convicted for 'particularly dangerous state crimes' (including those under article 70 of the RSFSR Criminal Code) or is a recidivist. In all other cases, if the convict lived in Moscow before and has relations there who are willing to take him, he can return. Thus in 1962 Ginzburg returned to Moscow after his first term of imprisonment and in 1969 Belogorodskaya returned – I mention those cases which are known in the West. Sometimes even a person convicted under article 70 of the Criminal Code may return. Thus in 1965 General Grigorenko returned to Moscow, released from Leningrad's psychiatric hospital prison. According to Mr Bradsher's logic, all of these are also agents of the KGB.

In the case of a change of review of sentence a return is even more obvious. There is no hope of a review of sentence and practically no hope of a return to Moscow in those cases where the authorities carry out an 'exposé' – with reports in the press, 'meetings of workers' and so on, as they did with Siniavsky and Daniel and Ginzburg and Galanskov. In the majority of ordinary cases, such as my own was in 1965, things are not quite like that. Mr Bradsher is on the whole badly informed about the law and judicial practice of the USSR, otherwise he would not have said that I wanted to 'test the law according to which the writers Andrei D. Siniavsky, Yuli Daniel and others were committed to prison for having sent their works abroad'. There is no law in the USSR forbidding one to send one's works abroad. Siniavsky and Daniel were formally convicted not for sending their works to the West but for their 'anti-Soviet character'. From this point of view it made no difference whether they published them in the West or circulated them in typescript among their friends in the USSR. By my publications I simply want to prove that, in the Soviet Union as well as in the West, there is no such law and that all prosecutions for this reason are illegal.

'Analysts found it curious', Mr Bradsher further writes, 'that both the 1965 arrest and the May raid [i.e. the search in 1969, *A.A.*] occurred in the presence of Americans . . .,' i.e. he wants to give his readers the impression that they were a special KGB fabrication. In reality I was arrested on 14 May 1965, without any witnesses; even my father, who was gravely ill, and my friends were only able to find out where I was after two weeks. If Mr Bradsher were really interested in the circumstances of my arrest and release, he would first have to read my book *Involuntary Journey to Siberia*, to which he refers in his article and where I wrote in detail about all this. I think that he would then refrain from his unpleasant and unproven assertions.

As for the search of 7 May 1969, it really took place in the presence of American correspondents and that, I think, gave the KGB no pleasure at all.

The third argument concerns my constant contact with foreigners and my friendly relations with certain American correspondents in Moscow. 'The dissenters, who have defended Daniel and Siniavsky, who publicly warned of a resurgence of Stalinism and who have denounced the invasion of Czechoslovakia,' Mr Bradsher writes, 'are able to do none of these. They are kept by the KGB from such familiarity with Westerners.'

Even according to Mr Bradsher's policeman's logic, one must assume that since these 'public protests and warnings' at any rate became known in the West and received wide publicity, some, if not all, of the 'genuine dissenters' must have had friendly and confidential relations with Westerners in Moscow, in as far as all *samizdat* gets to the West through channels other than Tass and Novosti.

In addition, one cannot draw this conclusion, since it is well known to Western journalists in Moscow that many dissenters have met and meet foreigners and both sides go to each other's houses.

I think that Mr Bradsher has drawn a rather distorted picture of the complete absence of contact between Russians and foreigners, because he himself during the four years of his work in Moscow never once spoke with a single Russian, except for officials, and what is more in general did not know a single word of Russian.

The KGB, indeed, hinders Soviet citizens' contacts with foreigners; in this they are helped by the 'super-wariness' of certain Western correspondents in Moscow, who are afraid to go beyond the four walls of their office and in every encounter with a Russian see 'an agent of the secret police'.

Mr Bradsher because of his gloomy suspicions allows himself other absurdities. He writes, for example, about how my wife and I were able to go on 4 July to a reception at the American Embassy when agents of the secret police were standing at the gates. We went in because we had an invitation, because of which no one would stop us. But we would generally be able to go in answer to any invitation, because, as Mr Bradsher must know well, at the beginning of the reception there are so many guests walking about that none of them is asked for his invitation and the KGB agents are simply not in a position to check on everyone.

Wishing at all costs to discredit me, Mr Bradsher is trying everything to cast me in a bad and distorted light, even using the fact that I like collecting paintings, whilst my wife, an artist, has sold some of her pictures to Americans. 'He has been a purveyor of underground art,' thus Mr Bradsher characterizes it. He tried 'to ingratiate himself with the wives of several successive American ambassadors', he warns later on.

In my opinion only a petty man could write in such a way.

The fourth argument is that my book *Will the Soviet Union Survive Until 1984?* is unpatriotic; I publicize myself through Western journalists, deceived by me, as 'a daring member ... of the band of dissenters'; Western radio stations broadcast the content of my book to Russian listeners; and all this transfers the indignation at my lack of patriotism on to the 'genuine dissenters'. This cunning plan was drawn up by the department of 'black propaganda' at Novosti, in which I worked, and was then unmasked by the anonymous 'defector from the USSR', who speaks according to Mr Bradsher as an expert on Russian patriotism.

I think that this plan is nevertheless too complicated for mere simple-minded people, who are concerned with Soviet propaganda and counter-propaganda; what is more, it would demand the cessation of the jamming of Western broadcasts, just for the narration of my book. But this is not the point.

Here, Mr Bradsher, as in the case of my letter to Kuznetsov, again resorts to direct falsification. I write that the sole hope of the whole world for the best future is not race war, but interracial cooperation, the best example of which would be cooperation between the USA and China; Mr Bradsher, in order to prove my 'anti-patriotism', represents this passage as a 'proposal for cooperation between the United States and China which would overthrow the Soviet system'. I wrote that in the event of a prolonged war with China in the border regions of the Soviet Union, tendencies towards national separation would make themselves felt more and more strongly; Mr Bradsher calls this 'an advocacy of regional nationalism in the Soviet Union'. Mr Bradsher also tries in every possible way to play up my work for the Novosti press agency, which is concerned mainly with propaganda in foreign countries. In fact I did work for them, as did thousands of other supernumerary journalists who do not undergo any special test. I interviewed Moscow producers and wrote articles about the theatre and painting; but as soon as the KGB again started taking an interest in me I was immediately dismissed from my work with Novosti, and they even refused to give a reference stating that I had worked for them for two years. After this, in order not to be expelled from Moscow again, I began distributing newspapers for the Post Office. One has to be endowed with a great imagination or a great lack of information in order to draw from this Mr Bradsher's conclusions.

So far as my 'anti-patriotism' is concerned, without distortion it is possible to find in my book harsh judgements about my country and about my people. It may be that the ordinary Russian, if he were given the opportunity to read or hear my book – and contrary to Mr Bradsher's opinion he will not be given such an opportunity – would find some passages in my book unpatriotic. But I consider that the best patriot is not the man who papers over his country's failings but the man who exposes the wounds so that they can be cured. It may be that it is unpatriotic to criticize one's country and to warn it of threatening dangers, publishing a book abroad for this purpose. But I have no other possibility. And besides, I consider that it is time for my country to overcome its national and social inferiority complex, which leads to every criticism from within or without being considered as something terrible.

I love my country, in which I was born and grew up, and I cannot think without tears of its extraordinary fate. To be separated from it would cause me great grief, but with bitterness I confess that I am not enraptured by my country. If I had been able to make a choice before my birth I should have preferred to be born in a small country fighting for its freedom with weapons in its hands, like Biafra or Israel.

The fifth argument is that, in spite of the publication of my books abroad, I have still not been arrested. My arrest is a kind of litmus paper which is to indicate whether I am a KGB agent or not. As far as I could understand, Mr Bradsher is not the only man who thinks like this.

To pose the question in such terms to me seems extremely immoral. My country is not a Roman arena. I am not a gladiator, and the Western world, in the name of which Mr Bradsher begins to speak with pathos towards the end of his article, is not the Roman plebs, watching excitedly or coolly to see whether the gladiator will really die or whether it is only a circus trick.

When I was writing my books and intending to hand them over for publication I realized that I was risking imprisonment, and I was ready for it and am ready for it now. But I thank God for every day of freedom which is given to me and which I spend at home with my wife. It seems to me that an honourable man who believes in God should not say: 'He has not yet been arrested – that is very suspicious,' but rather 'Thank God he has not yet been arrested, that means there is one more free man on earth.'

Mr Bradsher's anonymous 'specialists' have not, after all, occupied important positions in the secret police of a totalitarian state, and for this reason I think they are scarcely competent to judge who should be arrested straight away and who later. I think that the people in the KGB are reasonably sensible from the police point of view, and that they will arrest me when the fuss abroad has died down, and interest in me and my books has fallen away; and they will not try me for my books but will trump up some minor pretext. And before arresting me they will try to blacken my character as they tried to do with all the others. For this reason I think that Mr Bradsher's article will have delighted the KGB.

As far as the date of my arrest is concerned, a bureaucratic regime does not hurry by its very nature and because it knows that no one will escape it. Marchenko was arrested six months after he had begun circulating his book about Soviet prison camps; Grigorenko seven months after his famous speech at Kosterin's funeral; Bogoraz-Daniel and Litvinov seven months after their appeal 'To World Public Opinion'; Yakhimovich fourteen months after his letter to Suslov condemning the trials of dissenters; Gorbanyevskaya fifteen months after she had taken part in the demonstration in Red Square; and so on. I do not think that they have begun making an exception just for me.

In the West, moreover, the names are well known of Russian writers whose books have been published abroad, and many of whom nevertheless live in freedom; and it is certainly not necessary to commission a special agent to write books in order to 'soften the bad impression created abroad by the savagery of police repressions'.

There are many more inaccuracies in Mr Bradsher's article. He does not even know my name, calling me several times 'Andrei Aleksandrovish' instead of Andrei Alexeievich. But I think all this is not so important since I believe I have answered all his arguments. All except one, which seemed to me the most offensive.

'Amalrik's name was not found on any of the protests against the trial of Siniavsky and Daniel or the subsequent trials of young dissidents,' writes Mr Bradsher, and he draws the conclusion that I 'lack the confidence of other dissidents'.

It seems to me that he ought not to write in this way without knowing me and my friends personally. I am bound by ties of friendship, in some cases long-standing, to many of those who fought and are fighting for civil rights and freedom of speech in our country, and the majority of my friends have already paid for their struggle with imprisonment. My friends never doubted me, just as I did not doubt them. I hope that Mr Bradsher wrote this phrase in the heat of the moment, desiring, however he managed it, to give a basis to his suspicions, and that he now regrets it.

But, indeed, I never did sign any collective protests or requests directed mainly towards the Soviet authorities. I never joined any 'dissident group' and never professed to belong to any although I regard these people with great respect, am friendly with many of them, share their aims and try to be useful to them.

When I was finishing my book in a small Ryazan village and watching through the window how after light rain the goats grazed in melancholy fashion, I did not know if the book would ever be published, still less could I foresee that it would attract so much attention. But since this has happened, I wish to be correctly understood.

From childhood the regime under which I was compelled to live was organically alien to me: its culture seemed to be pitiful, its ideology false and the way of life foisted on my fellow-citizens humiliating. I am an individualist by nature and my protest has always been a personal one. I always wanted to uphold my human worth and the right to be free myself. But I do not want to be understood as always thinking only of myself. I would like – and perhaps my example helps here – each of my fellow-countrymen also to feel the significance of his own personality. Only then, I think, is a struggle for common interests possible.

85

Because a struggle for 'common interests' by people with a slave psychology can and does lead only to common slavery.

Therefore, I hope that I will be understood in America, a country created by freedom-loving individualists who have come from all corners of the world. I hope that my books, read not between the lines but exactly as I wrote them, will be the best answer to idle talk about them and to outright slander against me.

But if all the same this rumour sticks in the minds of my readers, I will at least be able to find comfort in the old Russian saying 'good repute lies under the pebbles while bad repute dashes along the path'.

A Letter to *Der Spiegel*

This letter appeared in Survey, *No. 74/75, and is reproduced by permission of the editor.*

Dear Editor,

I have read in your journal of 16 March 1970 an article about myself. It was not signed and therefore apparently expressed the view of your journal.

I was surprised that without offering any concrete evidence, you try to suggest to your readers that my book, *Will the Soviet Union Survive Until 1984?*, was written in collaboration with the KGB. Such rumours, as far as I know, first appeared in the American paper, the *Washington Evening Star*, in November last year. I wrote a detailed refutation which was published by some American and British papers to which you, while repeating some of the *Star* arguments, do not refer at all.

I will not try therefore to refute again in detail the slanderous innuendoes repeated by you that my return from exile and the publication of some of my articles by the Novosti Press Agency (whose regular employee I never was) had any relation to the KGB. In fact, the only relation to the KGB they had was that in 1965 the KGB exiled me to Siberia and in 1968 it put paid to my journalistic work for the Novosti Press Agency, and other Soviet publishing institutions.

All the same, I consider it necessary to reply to some of your allegations, because I think that they are dictated not by ill will, but simply by a complete lack of understanding of the conditions of Russian life.

Thus your comparisons between myself and Gapon and Malinovsky, or your suggestions that the purpose of my critical remarks about the Russian people was to sow discord between the people and the democratic opposition, are not just slanderous but simply nonsensical.

Unlike Gapon and Malinovsky, I am not a member of any organization, I am not trying to provoke anybody to collective action, I am expressing only my own personal views without trying to present them as opinions of the democratic opposition as a whole. As far as my sharp remarks about Russian history and the Russian people are concerned, I made them because I am Russian myself and think that at present my country is more in need of self-criticism than of self-praise.

Nor do I understand why you assert that my book was written for Western readers and that it is not being distributed by *samizdat*. I published the book first in the West and only afterwards I put it into *samizdat* circulation in order to avoid it being published [in a form which might have been distorted] by agencies which are not *bona fide* and which are beyond my control. But since the end of last year my book has had an extraordinarily wide distribution through *samizdat*.

Even more nonsensical and slanderous, not just personally to me, but to the whole of independent Russian literature, is the assertion by Mrs Bonska-Pampuch, approvingly quoted by you, that the sending of *samizdat* publications abroad is controlled, or even carried out, by the organs of the KGB. Apart from my writings, in the last few years there were published in the West the novels of Alexander Solzhenitsyn, the memoirs of Anatoly Marchenko, the poems of Natalya Gorbanyevskaya, the essays of Academician Sakharov and of General Grigorenko, the documentary compilations on political trials by Pavel Litvinov, and many other texts. Do you seriously think that all these were prepared or sent to the West on the initiative of the KGB?

It is true that the KGB has tried to pass to the West a few manuscripts, but only in such instances when it was against the wishes of the author, or could do him harm, as was the case with *The Banquet of the Victors* by Alexander Solzhenitsyn, or the diary of Svetlana Alliluyeva. But it would be simply dishonest to generalize from such cases.

In my view the KGB does not at all deserve the high marks which you give it in your article. Although the Committee of State Security is undoubtedly a more active and dynamic organization than – say – the Labour and Wages Committee, it is all the same a part of an ossified bureaucratic system and is affected by the general ways of its functioning. (You write that in my critique I do not include the KGB in the 'bureaucratic élite' which it merely supplies with information. Undoubtedly, the supplying of information about attitudes in the country is mainly the task of the KGB *apparatus,* but it does not follow that the top cadres of the KGB do not belong to the élite. Without wishing at all to underestimate the role of the KGB in the Soviet system – a role fully known only to a few people – I would like nevertheless to note that it is now not quite such an exceptional role as the one played by the secret police under Stalin.)

It is quite possible, as you write, that there are nowadays employed in the KGB well-educated and well-informed young men who 'have no illusion'. However, the clumsy provocations in which Victor Louis, whom you also mention, takes part, do not indicate high 'intellectual sophistication' on the part of the KGB. It would be too great an honour for the KGB to have such people as myself among its collaborators.

I think that the rumours that I am a KGB agent are spread by the KGB itself, perhaps partly through its own people in the Russian *émigré* organizations in the West. The purpose of these rumours is not only to slander me personally and thereby to harm my book which is embarrassing to the bureaucratic regime, but also to advertise the KGB as an organization which knows everything and controls everything.

Such rumours will undoubtedly meet with success among people whose mentality is conditioned by the awe felt *vis-à-vis* any organization (be it a national, party or police organization) and by those who, discounting individualism and human personality, believe in the strength of organizations, but not in the strength of man.

The fact that I have not yet been arrested is also used to support these rumours. I can only repeat here what I said before.

Will the Soviet Union Survive Until 1984?

After the propaganda failure suffered on the occasion of the Siniavsky–Daniel trial, the authorities do not want writers' trials which make a lot of noise, focus attention on their books and create a bad impression throughout the world of the authorities' cruelty. I am not the only Soviet writer who has published abroad and who nevertheless has not been arrested. The authorities are now more interested in the rumours that I am a KGB agent than in my arrest. But I think that as soon as the interest in the West in me and my writings passes, I will be arrested and tried on some false charge or other and that my writings will not even be mentioned at the trial. Of course, they may deal with me in some other way too.

So far, however, I am in fact enjoying greater freedom than many Soviet citizens. But I owe this only to myself. *I want to be free.* It is precisely because of this that I act as any free man can and should act: I publish my books under my own name and I want to enjoy all the rights of an author. Even in prison, if they do put me in prison, I hope to remain more free than millions of my and your compatriots who in their time, while 'free', shouted 'hurrah' to Stalin and Hitler and believed in the omnipotence of the organizations created by them.

I hope that you will publish my letter in full in your journal.

Andrei Amalrik
2 April 1970

An Author's Fight for Rights

The following letter was sent in December 1969 to the editors of The Times *which published it on December 1969, the* New York Times, Le Monde *(Paris),* Het Parool *(Netherlands), the* Washington Post *and the* Los Angeles Times. *It was reprinted in the American edition of* Will the Soviet Union Survive Until 1984? *(Harper & Row, 1971).*

Dear Mr Editor:

Several publishing houses in Holland, the United States of America, Britain and France either have published or are publishing my books *An Involuntary Journey to Siberia* and *Will the Soviet Union Survive Until 1984?* and also my plays. I have made contracts, either directly or through the person whom I have authorized to act on my behalf, with all these publishing houses.

In addition to my desire to publish my books, I have wanted also to prove that a Soviet citizen, like the citizen of any other country, has the right to publish books not issued in his own country, to do this under his own name, to fix personally with the publishers the terms of publication, and to enjoy all author's rights which flow from this.

One of these rights is to receive royalties. Several publishing houses have in fact already sent off to me via the Soviet State Bank part of the royalties on my books. However, the official Soviet bodies which control the exchange of foreign currency are in fact preventing me from receiving these royalties.

Referring to a secret instruction, they have stated that I publish my books in the West without the agreement of Soviet official bodies, hence illegally, and so the rules about the handing over of authors' royalties will not be extended to cover my case. At best they are ready to regard my royalties as a 'present', which has been sent to me by someone in the West.

Such an attitude is unacceptable to me, inasmuch as the royalties are not a present but money I have earned. Evidently, however, the attitude is advantageous to the Soviet Government, because a present is subject to a much higher tax than a royalty. In the All-Union Office for the Defence of Authors' Rights, to which I turned for help, they told me that all my publications are absolutely legal, but they refused to help me in defending my rights.

Three years ago I wanted to give to Florence, which had suffered from floods, the royalties on a book of my father's published in the Soviet Union, which I was entitled to do as his heir. The Soviet Ministry of Finance refused to let me do this, referring to the fact that the Soviet Government is extremely short of foreign currency and cannot therefore convert Soviet roubles into such currency.

Bearing in mind this serious situation of the Soviet Government, I would be able to donate to it a certain sum in foreign currency, but I will never do this under compulsion. Therefore if my author's rights are not going to be respected in the Soviet Union, I will be forced to ask my publishers not to send royalties through official bodies as unreliable as Soviet ones, but rather to keep them in the West.

I ask your respected newspaper to publish my letter so that I may publicly shame the Soviet Government for the meanness and pettiness which it has shown. While Stalin would have shot me for publishing my books abroad, his pitiful heirs are only up to trying to appropriate a part of my money. This confirms my view about the degeneration and growing decrepitude of this regime, which I have expounded in the book *Will the Soviet Union Survive Until 1984?*.

Respectfully yours,

Andrei Amalrik

Foreign Correspondents in Moscow

This article, written in April 1970, was published (in slightly shortened form) in English translation in the New York Review of Books *on 25 March 1971.*

The wife of an American correspondent in Moscow invited a young Russian friend into her home. At the gates of the house they were stopped by a policeman. Addressing the American woman he said: 'You go ahead. But as for you', said the policeman, pulling the Russian by the arm, 'go back.'

The American woman tried to protest but the young man immediately began to walk away with a frightened expression on his face.

'Why didn't you lodge a complaint against the policeman?' I asked the correspondent's wife after she had recounted the incident. 'Whom should I complain to?' she replied. 'The press department of MID (Ministry of Foreign Affairs) is already persistently warning us not to associate with Russians other than official persons.'

This minor episode is perhaps very characteristic of the situation of foreign correspondents in Moscow, and of their own attitude. Although the 'iron curtain' concept now seems very old-fashioned, the authorities are still striving to isolate foreign correspondents in Moscow completely from Soviet citizens. This situation existed earlier, but more resolute measures have been taken to isolate the correspondents ever since the beginning of an independent opposition movement within the country. It is clear that the whole world could have learned about this movement only from the information of Western correspondents in Moscow (and in the USSR, from foreign radio broadcasts), for neither TASS nor any other Soviet organ would ever have publicized it. However, this is naturally not simply a question of the movement: in general, a man isolated from the local population has far less understanding of what is going on in the country.

The government isolates correspondents first and foremost by settling them into special apartments for foreigners, to which Soviet citizens do not have easy access; by creating establishments to cater especially to foreigners; by setting up microphones in the correspondents' apartments; by having them followed (which tends to make those unaccustomed to this very nervous); by a system of official and non-official warnings; by expulsion from the country; and also by creating a general atmosphere of fear and uncertainty which is particularly painful to those who come from democratic countries.

Many of the journalists who enter into discourse exaggerating the 'liberalization and democratization of Soviet society' tend equally to exaggerate the threat to which they personally are exposed.

The correspondents ostensibly write about their own situation in Moscow. However, the opinion of a detached onlooker is perhaps also of interest, and especially his assessment of the correspondents' behaviour in such a situation.

There are clearly two choices: the correspondents can either seek contact of some kind with Russians, and hunt for some sort of information other than the official; or they can fully accept the status to which the Moscow authorities have tied them down with a firm or gentle hand. After seven years of continual contact with foreign correspondents, I have formed the impression that the majority of them display a readiness to submit to these imposed conditions.

As long as the correspondent is not engaged in any reporting work and the gathering of facts; as long as he has no understanding or awareness of the general situation; as long as he continues to move in the narrow circle of his own people, with no knowledge of Russian history or traditions and, in most cases, even of the Russian language, his work is reduced to the following: A Soviet interpreter, whom the correspondent himself regards as a KGB agent, either translates or relates to him the contents of *Pravda* or *Krasnaya zvezda*, i.e. the 'official view' of a certain event. The correspondent then chats with a neighbour on the same floor, who is just like himself and has an 'observer's' point of view. In certain particularly important cases he questions his chauffeur or domestic help, for the opinion of the 'man in the street'.

Now it only remains for him to discuss the contents of *Pravda* in Western journalistic terms, adding trite remarks about 'liberalization' or on the contrary, the 'rebirth of Stalinism'. Thus emerge articles about 'economic reforms' or the 'hawks and doves in the Kremlin', full of false significance and lacking any content, articles which could have been written just as successfully in London or New York as in Moscow. However, the label 'from our Moscow correspondent' perhaps lends a fascination to news from the actual place of the event, and enhances the newspaper's prestige.

The correspondent, who, after three or four years in Russia, has not learned a word of the language, and has never spoken to a single Russian, returns to his country, where he is regarded as a 'Russian expert'. He writes articles which may be either extremely hostile or very well-disposed towards the Soviet regime, but which are invariably liable to mislead the reader, since their author possesses very little knowledge and even less understanding.

At present more and more Soviet citizens feel the burden of their isolation from the rest of the world, and are themselves seeking contact with foreigners, including foreign correspondents. However, these attempts to 'break down the barrier' come up not only against opposition from the KGB, but against the prejudices of the correspondents themselves, who feel that every Russian who wishes to associate with them is overtly or covertly a KGB agent. This 'spy-mania' is perhaps caused by three circumstances: first of all, agents may indeed be sent to correspondents; secondly, it might seem strange to the correspondents that certain Russians are not afraid to meet them, when they themselves are afraid, though exposed to a far smaller degree of personal risk. Finally, a correspondent's own situation seems far better justified when, instead of going to see some dubious Russian friends, he goes without bothering to take off his slippers from his apartment on the second floor to the office on the third, to take a look at the reliable TASS teletypes.

However, even as he acknowledges this idyllic way of life, such a correspondent for some reason considers himself almost a James Bond who is permanently exposed to a terrible risk, a 'risk' which is for the most part imaginary. There is, in fact, no written law prohibiting contact between Soviet citizens and foreigners, and however dim a view of such contact the authorities may choose to take, they are nevertheless obliged to tolerate it when it occurs. In fact, the only way to prevent this is by means of blackmail; however, submission to blackmail is not a compulsory, but a voluntary matter.

Nevertheless, some correspondents do occasionally enter into contact with Soviet citizens, and even seek contacts for themselves. Unfortunately, however, they do not always display sufficient tact in their attitude towards these Russians.

Following the trial of Ginzburg and Galanskov (in 1968), Ginzburg's mother and Galanskov's wife arranged to meet a few foreign correspondents at the home of L. I. Ginzburg, in order to relate the course of the trial. However, at the appointed time nobody turned up. The house was instead surrounded by KGB agents, and the two women seemed to be trapped.

It later appeared that the MID (Ministry of Foreign Affairs) press department, after learning about the meeting from correspondents, had flatly refused to allow anyone to visit L. I. Ginzburg. The MID press department referred not to any law or instruction, but simply hinted that things 'will be very unpleasant for anybody who should go to see her'. This apparently not only sufficed to prevent the correspondents from going there, but also prevented those who had promised to come from giving Ginzburg and Galanskov any advance warning.

The KGB arranged a provocation against the two women, who had known nothing of all this: first of all they tried to lure them out of their house ostensibly to a meeting in the street with some correspondents, only in order to accuse them later of illegal street assembly; when this attempt failed, Vasily Gritsan, a KGB agent, presented himself to them in the guise of a foreign correspondent. Had one of the foreign correspondents out of a simple sense of decency warned these women by phone that nobody would be coming, both of them would have been delivered from a real and not just an imaginary danger.

Nevertheless, a few correspondents whom the MID press department did not manage to notify arrived at Ginzburg's home. KGB agents did not allow them near the house, telling them to return to their offices to look for the belated note prohibiting them from attending the press conference, which they would find in their post boxes. There were three Swedish correspondents among them, and the KGB agent sternly inquired whether they had arrived for the Ginzburg press conference, to which the frightened Swedes replied: 'No, no, we are simply taking a walk here.'

Perhaps they considered their reply exceptionally clever but, in my opinion, it was more the retort of a mischievous schoolboy than the reply of adult journalists whose right and duty it was to attend that press conference which would be of interest to their readers.

On the eve of the Moscow local elections, while strolling along the Arbat, I saw on the walls of several houses the portrait of a none-too-intelligent-looking man with a coarse and fierce expression. This was Leonid Zamyatin, the only official candidate for our district. In this way I at least discovered the appearance of the man whose name was continually being pronounced with fear and awe by journalists, like Jews uttering the Lord's name.

Mr Zamyatin heads the MID press department, which I have already mentioned, and which supervises the work of Moscow's foreign correspondents. This surveillance and the supervisor's relationship with the correspondents not only involve their written work but also extend to their personal contacts and whereabouts.

Various degrees of pressure are brought to bear on an unwelcome journalist. For example, he may be caused various everyday inconveniences. The correspondent who is living in a hotel may be informed that he must alter the tone of his articles if he wishes to receive an apartment sooner. The authorities may make the journalist's access to information more difficult. They may refuse him a meeting with an official writer or actor, or forbid him to go to any other town. They may speak critically of him in *Pravda* or *Izvestia*, or he may be summoned to the MID press department for a warning. They may simply tell him not to write about this or that, for it is not a normal phenomenon of Soviet life, and he has to be objective. Or that he must not have anything to do with so-and-so, who is a man with a shady past.

However, they may also issue an 'official warning' which, if the correspondent chooses to ignore it, could lead to his expulsion or even to a threat to close down the newspaper's Moscow office or agency. Warnings of this sort tend to be very crude and direct. Thus, Anatol Shub, correspondent for the *Washington Post*, mentioned in an article that a 'Russian friend' of his was preparing to write a book entitled *Will the Soviet Union Survive Until 1984?* and included a summary of his friend's opinions. 'No Soviet man could have said that! Your "Russian friend" was the bottle of vodka over which you chatted, after having first of all emptied it!' the press department announced to Shub. 'If you write anything more like this you will be expelled from Moscow!'

It should be said that such warnings were not just empty words. Shub was subsequently expelled from the USSR.

Occasionally correspondents attempt to clarify the grounds on which the press department issues one prohibition or another, but they are told that there are special instructions which, incidentally, are not shown to anyone. It is quite possible that the press department periodically 'unleashes' (as they say in our country) official instructions of one kind or another compulsory only for itself, and not for actual foreign journalists. In fact there exists an officially printed document determining the foreign correspondent's position and defining his rights and duties in this country. Uncertain conditions such as these obviously suit the authorities for they allow them freedom to manoeuvre as they wish. So using their own sense of reason, the courage which every man possesses, and even emulating the way in which 'others behave', the correspondents strive to adjust, in conditions which inevitably lead to a certain confusion.

Thus, some feel that they are able to visit Russians, but that they themselves ought not to invite Russians into their homes; others, on the contrary, feel that they can invite Russians into their apartments while they ought not to visit them in their own homes. Some think that they can bravely criticize the regime as long as they are not within their office walls; others feel that they must write favourable articles, for only then will they be given the opportunity to see more. The basic tendency, i.e. the less one does, the better one lives, somewhat contradicts the journalists' professional obligations.

As I gathered from my talks with journalists, many are themselves aware of the abnormality of their position in Moscow. Nevertheless, scarcely any of them wished to defend his rights, on the assumption that this would only anger the Soviet authorities even further. Foreign correspondents in Moscow to this day still do not possess a union or club of their own, and completely lack any notion of professional association. As a rule, when a conflict arises between the authorities and a correspondent, not only do they fail to unite in defence of the latter and his violated rights, but they occasionally even experience a gloating feeling of satisfaction. There you are, I told you to be more careful. I haven't written or done anything, and they are not expelling me!

This kind of dissociation proves how rapidly people confronted by a totalitarian regime begin to accept its rules, for the fundamental rule of any such regime is to deal with each man separately. Totalitarianism fears nothing so much as united opposition. I do not wish people to feel that I am calling upon Western journalists to struggle against the Soviet regime, for I simply have in mind their united struggle for their own professional rights within the limits of present Soviet law.

Incidentally, in order to remain objective, I ought to mention a case where correspondents did in fact come out *in corpore* in defence of their own rights. This happened when they had been refused permission to order goods from abroad.

99

As I have already stated, the foreign correspondents in Moscow are controlled by the press department of the MID and the KGB, not in accordance with the law, but according to considerations of the present moment and by means of blackmail. Naturally, the greater the readiness to submit, the more successful the blackmail, whereas if it meets with opposition the blackmail can easily prove entirely fruitless. It is generally known that there are several journalists who displayed sufficient firmness and prudence, did not allow themselves to be intimidated, and by continuing to write objective articles revealed the situation in the USSR to the Western world. True, a number of them were expelled, but by no means all. If other journalists would react negatively to warnings and expulsions of this sort, and if foreign states would place Soviet journalists under similar conditions, then this would serve to alter radically the Moscow correspondents' situation.

Naturally, the present situation could not exist without the direct or indirect collaboration of several correspondents with the Soviet authorities.

Normally the authorities try to avoid extending the correspondent's visa for longer than a period of three to four years, realizing that the longer he stays the better he will come to appreciate the situation, and the harder it will be to deceive him. Nevertheless, there are several correspondents in Moscow whose length of stay may now be calculated not in years but in decades, and these are no longer prevented from freely associating with Russians.

One of them is —, head of the Moscow office of —. Having lived in Moscow for thirty years, he is considered an expert on Russian life. However, when this same Mr — received a copy of the famous essay by Academician Sakharov, the 'father of the Soviet hydrogen bomb,' after taking just one look at it, he immediately hid it in his desk, declaring that its existence ought not to be disclosed for fear of major unpleasantness. Nevertheless, Sakharov's *Reflections on Progress* acquired worldwide fame. First of all an abridged text of the article was handed over to the Moscow correspondent of the newspaper *Het Parol*, Mr Van Het Reve, after which the complete text appeared in the *New York Times*. The significance which was attached in the West to Sakharov's address is generally known. However, had all the correspondents acted in the same way as Mr —, to this day nobody would have heard anything about the article.

Deliberate silence may also result in the direct distortion of fact. Thus, after the Ginzburg and Galanskov press conference which failed to take place, Mr — pointed out that there was a 1947 decree which prohibited foreigners from associating with Soviet citizens. This decree, which had in fact long since been obsolete, had served to establish an order of official relations between Soviet institutions and the corresponding institutions of other countries. By means of such misrepresentation Mr — was seeking to mislead other correspondents while at the same time justifying the illegal activities of the MID press department.

Naturally, 'good behaviour' such as this deserves rewards, which are exactly what the authorities offer. Reward involves first and foremost access to information in one form or another. Victor Louis, correspondent to the English newspaper *Evening News*, about whose special relations with the Soviet authorities much has already been written, at his villa 30 kilometres from Moscow was able to learn the verdict of the Ginzburg and Galanskov affair before the journalists who were standing in the entrance to the courtroom knew of it.

Very frequently the newspapers and agencies account for this kind of silence and distortion by alluding to the huge interests of their newspaper or agency and the danger that their Moscow bureau might be completely closed down by the authorities. Obviously, there is a certain amount of logic in this; however, the real problem is where to draw a reasonable line. If offices are simply going to communicate the leading articles of *Pravda* as the authorities would like them to do, then their work will be meaningless.

The more concessions the head of such an office begins to make, the greater are the demands laid upon him. At times the MID press department delivers even stricter warnings to those correspondents who are 'in good repute'. Thus, Mr — was the only correspondent to have received a warning for having been seen at the building where Pavel Litvinov was standing trial.

By no means do I wish to create the impression that all foreign correspondents are like the ones I have described here. I have not mentioned several correspondents whose objectivity merits the utmost respect, simply because any praise on my part would impede their work, for it would serve as poor recommendation in the eyes of the authorities.

However, the general situation does not seem at all normal to me. The Soviet authorities continue their slow but persistent manipulation of information coming from Moscow. The Western reader is the one who loses the most by this, since the information which he receives about the Soviet Union is distorted. It is therefore mainly for the sake of these readers that I have written this article.

Amalrik on Trial in Sverdlovsk: Statement in Court and Final Plea

Amalrik was arrested in May 1970 and brought to trial on 11 November 1970 in the city of Sverdlovsk in the Urals, about 1,000 miles east of Moscow, the remote location of the proceedings being clearly designed to divert foreign interest and make it impossible for Western correspondents in Moscow to attend. Amalrik was charged under Article 190–1 of the Criminal Code with having written and circulated 'slanderous fabrications' including his essay Will the Soviet Union Survive Until 1984? Involuntary Journey to Siberia *(which described the time he spent in Siberia working in exile in 1965–6 under the parasite law), the 'Letter to Anatoly Kuznetsov', and also with having given interviews to foreign correspondents, in particular in a film shown on American television on 28 July 1970 and in Britain on 28 August of the same year (for the complete text of which see* Survey, *No. 77, 1970). At his trial, Amalrik refused to recognize the legitimacy of the charge or indeed of the court itself and submitted the statement below to the court chairman. His defence counsel Vladimir Shveisky, a noted defender of dissidents, asked for an acquittal; however, Amalrik was sentenced to three years in a hard-regime corrective labour camp after making a short final plea.*

The text of the 'Statement in court' is taken from Chronicle of Current Events, *No. 17, 30 December 1970; English edition published by Amnesty International. The text of the 'final plea' (12 November 1970) is reprinted from the same source.*

Statement in court

The charges brought against me concern the dissemination by me, verbally and in print, of views which are here called false and slanderous. I do not consider either the interview given by me or my articles and books to be slanderous.

I also think that the truth or falseness of publicly expressed views can be ascertained by free and open discussion, but not by a judicial investigation. No criminal court has the moral right to try anyone for the views he has expressed. To oppose ideas – irrespective of whether they are true or false – with a judicial criminal penalty seems to me to be a crime in itself.

This point of view is not only natural for everyone who has his own opinions and who needs creative freedom; it also finds legal expression both in the Constitution of the USSR and in the Universal Declaration of Human Rights, which all the signatory-nations have promised to put into effect.

Thus as a man to whom creative freedom is essential, and as the citizen of a country which has signed the Universal Declaration of Human Rights, I consider that this court is not entitled to try me, and therefore I shall not enter into any discussion of my views with the court, I shall not give any evidence and I shall not answer any of the court's questions. I do not plead guilty to circulating 'falsehood and slanderous fabrications', and I shall not attempt to prove my innocence here, since the very principle of freedom of speech excludes the possibility of my guilt.

If during the trial I wish to add anything to what I have said, I shall avail myself of my right to make a final address.

Final plea

The criminal prosecution of people for their statements or opinions reminds me of the middle ages with their 'witch trials' and indexes of forbidden books. But if the medieval struggle against heretical ideas could be partially explained by religious fanaticism, everything that is happening now is due only to the cowardice of a regime which perceives danger in the dissemination of any thought or any idea alien to the upper strata of the bureaucracy.

These people understand that the collapse of any regime is preceded by its ideological capitulation. But, while holding forth about an ideological struggle, they can in reality oppose ideas only with the threat of criminal prosecution. Conscious of their ideological helplessness, they clutch fearfully at the criminal code, prisons, camps and psychiatric hospitals.

It is precisely this fear of the thoughts I have expressed, and of the facts I adduce in my books, which forces these people to put me in the dock like a criminal. This fear has reached such proportions that they were even afraid to try me in Moscow and brought me here, calculating that here my trial would attract less attention.

But it is just these manifestations of fear which prove best of all the strength and correctness of my opinions. My books will be none the worse for the abusive epithets with which they have here been described. The opinions I have expressed will not become less correct if I am imprisoned for a few years because of them. On the contrary, this can only impart greater strength to my convictions. The trick which says that people are tried not for their convictions but for circulating them seems to me to be empty sophistry, since convictions which do not manifest themselves in any way are not genuine convictions.

As I have already said, I shall not here enter into a discussion of my opinions, since a court is not the place for that. I wish only to answer the assertion that several of my statements are directed against my people and my country. It seems to me that my country's principal task at present is to throw off the burden of its hard past, for which, above all, it needs criticism and not eulogies. I think I am a better patriot than those who loudly hold forth about love for their country, meaning by that – love for their own privileges.

Neither the 'witch-hunt' conducted by the regime nor this trial – an individual example of it – produces in me the slightest respect, nor even fear. I understand, of course, that trials like this are calculated to intimidate many, and many will be intimidated – but I still think that the process of ideological liberation which has now begun is irreversible.

I have no requests to make of the court.

The appeal of Amalrik's lawyer to the RSFSR Supreme Court was quashed on 9 February 1971. In March he began the long journey to his camp in Kolyma in north-west Siberia, near Magadan on the Sea of Okhotsk. En route he was taken ill with meningitis and was near to death for several days. He did not reach his camp at Talaya until the end of June, after three months in transit prisons, hospitals and solitary cells. Throughout his term there was serious concern for his health. On the very day on which he was scheduled for release (in May 1973) he was charged yet again under the same Article 190–1, tried in Magadan in July 1973 and sentenced to a further three years' imprisonment. After a 117-day hunger strike the sentence was commuted to one of exile and his wife was allowed to join him in Magadan. Only in May 1975 was he able to return to Moscow and, once returned, severe restrictions were placed on his movements.

The West, Détente and the USSR

After his return from exile in May 1975, Amalrik resumed his publicist activity, this time turning to the theme of East–West relations in the light of the policy of détente and the drawing up of the Helsinki Agreements, one of which contained guarantees for the observance of democratic human rights in the signatory states, including the Soviet Union.

The first article, 'Are the USA and the USSR in the Same Boat?', was written in August 1975 while Amalrik was living in a small provincial town outside Moscow since the police had refused him permission to live with his wife in their apartment in the capital. The article appeared in a slightly abbreviated English translation in the New York Times of 22 October 1975. The version published here is the full text.

The four articles which I have combined under this heading were written between August 1975 and December 1976, during what I would call the year of the West's disillusionment with détente.

When I wrote my first article, at a time when expectations from détente were at their highest, I had no doubt that disillusionment would inevitably follow – but even so I did not think it would set in so soon. However, I do not overestimate the significance of this disillusionment.

Disillusionment with détente is a consequence of political realism; it demands changes in policy, but these require moral strength and political will. Détente is a consequence of the desire to see things as you want to see them, and all you have to do in order to carry it through is to accept the world as it is. It is not difficult to guess that a policy requiring the minimum of effort will attract the maximum support. Putting it crudely, the West is sitting too easily to stand firmly.

Meanwhile, refusal to take a moral stand, political limpness and the tendency to regard dictatorship as something 'natural' for non-Western peoples may lead rather rapidly to the disintegration of the Western democracies themselves. The success of totalitarianism in one place encourages it to rear its head in another.

By its political overtures and economic aid the West hopes to 'soften up' the Soviet Union; in so doing, however, it is fostering not only a hostile state but the very idea of totalitarianism. Of course, each of the Western countries has its own rational or irrational reasons for its actions. Britain's attitude to the USSR contains, as I see it, the barely perceptible imprint of its past: a former empire, Britain unconsciously continues to respect imperial power and to despise colonial peoples; hence its respect for the power of the Russians and its contempt for them as a people.

Andrei Amalrik
June 1977

Are the USA and the USSR
in the Same Boat?

It took the United States sixteen years (1917–33) to grant the USSR diplomatic recognition, eight years (1933–41) to become its ally, four years (1941–5) to make a joint effort with the USSR to reorganize the world, but only two (1945–7) to become thoroughly disillusioned with that policy.

Why was the US so slow to recognize the USSR? Diplomatic recognition, after all, does not mean approval, and non-recognition does not of itself force a revolutionary regime to change in a desired direction. Why did the US miss the opportunity to support moderate elements in the USSR, by failing to recognize it during the NEP[1] period but recognizing it instead at a time of mass repressions? Why did the US plunge headlong into rapprochement with the USSR, only to pull up to a sudden, stupefied halt?

Probably because the US had little interest in Soviet internal problems. America's foreign policy line was determined by whatever forces there gained the upper hand; it could be tragically inappropriate to what was happening in the Soviet Union.

Franklin D. Roosevelt's policy of rapprochement with the USSR was evidently based not only on the dictates of wartime but also on the more general view that world stability was impossible without the inclusion of the USSR in a world system. Within a stable world system the USSR seemed to Roosevelt less dangerous than outside it, and, hence, instead of paying to join the system, the USSR was itself paid, in the first instance by being granted the right to a free hand in Eastern Europe.

Where indeed is it better to have a destructive sub-system – within a system or outside it? For, as experience has shown, inclusion in the system does not *per se* transform the sub-system from a destructive to a constructive one. Putting it another way, if we imagine the Western countries as the oarsmen of a boat and the USSR as a swimmer, is it more sensible to invite the USSR into the boat in the hope that it will pull together with everyone else instead of rocking the boat, or to keep the USSR out of the boat, fearing that it may sink it but at the same time hoping that, alone, it will sooner or later exhaust its strength?

Roosevelt invited Stalin into the boat. Alas, the gesture altered neither the domestic nor the foreign policy of the USSR. Stalin not only rocked the boat but, figuratively speaking, jumped out of it himself. Feeling it had been made a fool of and acknowledging its responsibility for 'foisting communism' upon Eastern Europe, the United States switched abruptly to a policy of 'containment of communism', not only protecting the remainder of Europe but, most importantly, resolved now not to give up Asia without a fight. However, here too the US was once again inclined to ignore the attitude of the peoples themselves to 'Communism'.

Failure to understand processes in progress in other countries made the US over-reliant on manipulation by military strength and economic assistance. If we take the view that the communist revolutions in Asia were the result of the historical development of those countries and that 'communism' there became a form of budding Asian nationalism and egalitarianism, and was in no way a consequence of Soviet intrigues, we may consider post-war American policy in Asia just as unfortunate as American policy in Europe during the war.

Had the US recognized the Chinese People's Republic in 1949, not only would the Korean War have been avoided but China's break with the USSR would have happened sooner. The creation of a potential threat in the East would have made the USSR more pliant in the West: in all probability the USSR, without a friendly China at its back, would have agreed in 1953 to the reunification of Germany. However, the United States not only did not recognize China but resolved to attack 'communism' in an area where it was itself most vulnerable – Vietnam, where the regime it supported solely because it was

'anti-communist' was viewed by the Vietnamese people themselves as the heir to a colonial regime and was therefore doomed
to fall.

Somewhere between the two crises – the United States' disillusionment with the 'encouragement of communism' in Europe
at the end of the forties and its disappointment with the 'containment of communism' in Asia at the beginning of the seventies
– there began what is now termed the 'politics of détente' and was
earlier called the 'politics of peaceful coexistence'. Despite its
growing military might, the boat of Stalinism with an indigent
China at the stern and untrustworthy East Europeans at the
prow was scarcely suitable for ramming the Western vessel. The
Soviet Union's isolation during the last years of Stalin's life had
overtaxed the country's strength and led to a series of convulsive
reforms in the fifties. Thus it was only after having experienced
all the negative aspects of isolation taken to extremes that the
USSR embarked on a course of domestic transformations and
the cultivation of foreign relations.

The US, weary of the 'cold war' and the strain associated with
it, met the USSR half-way, albeit with reservations. Most probably the US overestimated the changes that had occurred in the
USSR since Stalin's death. In addition, the emergence of a new
political 'continent', the Third World, influenced the thinking of
the American and Soviet leadership, giving an impulse to both
competition and cooperation.

The removal of Kennedy and Khrushchev coincided with a
more sceptical attitude to détente. The United States became
involved in the Vietnamese conflict, while in the USSR isolationist ideas came to the fore and prevailed once again for
several years.

However, the objective course of history proved more powerful. If the US had already attained the level of a power which
aspired not to change anything in the world but to preserve what
already existed, the USSR too had gradually begun to approach
that level. There was bound to be a certain point at which the
need for an understanding would inevitably arise.

The objectivity of this rapprochement is most clearly visible from the fact that this time it was presided over by rather featureless figures who had earlier displayed nothing but hostility towards any system other than their own. However, it was precisely the fact that each of them was first and foremost the protégé of his own bureaucratic apparatus which helped them to draw closer together and to understand one another better.

Assessing the advantages of détente over the cold war, we don't have the right, it seems, to say that détente is the alternative to war. The cold war, being a form of sublimation of hot war, was not less effective than 'détente' in averting a real war, because peace depended, and still depends, on the balance of nuclear power. Therefore, even a mutual reduction of weapons, should it ever be achieved, would not reduce and would not increase the risks of war.

The rise in armaments is a consequence of confrontation, not its cause, and to a certain degree is a consequence of scientific–technical progress. Inasmuch as an accord about reductions in these or those areas will not end either confrontation or progress, the arms race if suppressed in one area will merely emerge in another. A reduction in arms may be a result of détente but it is not its sole nor basic content. Therefore, it is better to look upon détente as an instrument not for the safeguarding of peace but rather for the improvement of the world. Otherwise, there would be no sense in détente.

An impression is growing, however, that the objective of the US in détente is precisely the safeguarding of the existing situation. It seems to be striving to entangle the USSR in a web of treaties and mutual commitments, and thereby deprive it of the ability to disrupt world stability without concern that these ties might be severed.

For the USSR, the side still on the offensive, the objectives of détente are much broader. The USSR is striving to emerge from isolation for at least three reasons: first, to use détente with the West to manipulate the Western countries one by one rather than in a group, and this is already happening to a certain extent: second, to assure itself of a secure rear in view of the hostile relations with China; third, to overcome the economic backwardness deriving from the isolation.

Despite important military–industrial achievements, the economy of the USSR remains bogged down and needs technological and organizational modernization, and this is impossible without assistance from the West. In addition, the backward state of agriculture compels the USSR to buy grain regularly in the West. Two bad harvests in succession without such purchases could shake the Soviet economy and even provoke mass upheavals.

Further, détente is explained, as I see it, by two not fully clear but real circumstances: first, by the fact that the US and the USSR regard each other as the only equal partners; second that they along with other developed countries are beginning to consider themselves not only rivals but also to a certain degree as allies – somewhat like a group of well-fed in a crowd of hungry.

I speak of these tendencies recognizing that opposing tendencies are at work and that the USSR remains in the eyes of the US as before, a destructive force. Whether or not the American leaders recognize it, a fundamental change in the foreign policy of the USSR is impossible without a change in its internal situation.

It is difficult to imagine a state combining constant suppression and violence internally with peaceful behaviour and accommodation externally. Such 'peaceful behaviour' could only be the consequence of military weakness or of deceptive camouflage. Therefore, any relaxation in the internal policies of the USSR should be desirable to the Americans not only out of humanitarian considerations. It is also vitally important to them for reasons of their own security, and therefore can be regarded as one of the objectives of US policy.

Since the US in working out its political strategy, chose cooperation with the USSR rather than its isolation, two tactical variations were possible:

1. To move towards *rapprochement*, expecting that the cooperation of the US and the West in general would gradually 'soften' the USSR.

2. To tie every step towards the USSR to a demand for a particular change in both internal and external policies, understanding their interdependency.

An impression has been created that Richard M. Nixon and Henry A. Kissinger chose the first path as the one seemingly requiring less effort and giving visible results promptly. Mr Kissinger sought to resolve in barely two years the challenge of *rapprochement* with the USSR, a task requiring, let us say, two decades. Such haste possibly reflects not only the mentality of Mr Kissinger himself but also the features of American mentality in general – the mentality of businessmen who want to see at once the tangible results of their efforts.

This led the American Government to the hasty signing of a series of agreements only for the purpose of presenting them to the citizens on television and saying: 'Look! We have done this and this and this!' But the US is dealing with a partner with which it is dangerous to make haste. Even if the Soviet leaders do not possess the many brilliant qualities of Mr Kissinger, they are able to a superlative degree to set themselves distant goals and also to wait patiently.

American policy differs from Soviet policy in two other features. Foreign policy in a way is a pupil of internal policy. The mentality of government officials rising to foreign policy leadership has been shaped for years by dealing with internal political problems, and all the methods they have mastered inside the country are applied abroad.

American domestic policies are based on a play of free forces, settled by compromise, while Soviet domestic policies are based on a no-compromise implementation of instructions. And while the US may sit down at the negotiating table consciously or subconsciously thinking of compromise, the USSR sits down with the intention of achieving its objectives in full agreeing only to fictitious concessions.

The other strange feature of American policy, as with the policy of the West in general, is the treatment of the USSR like a small child who must be allowed everything and not be irritated because he might start screaming – all because, they say, when it grows up it will understand everything.

This prolonged 'upbringing' of the USSR by the methods of Dr Spock is reflected not only in an endless number of minor concessions by the US but also in actions that are simply humiliating for its prestige as a big power. This was most clearly illustrated by the reluctance of President Ford to invite Alexander I. Solzhenitsyn to the White House because Mr Kissinger feared this would infuriate Leonid I. Brezhnev.

Such behaviour in general is very typical for representatives of the American Government. Thus, an American diplomat with whom I have been acquainted for more than ten years and who recently returned to Moscow declined for the same reasons to meet with me, although he did send expressions of his sympathy via an intermediary.

Knowing the character of those whom the Americans are trying to play up to by such behaviour, I believe that even though it wins approval from their side it also arouses a degree of contempt. The whole situation reminds one of the relationship between the shopkeeper and the vandal: the shopkeeper cringes before the vandal lest the vandal prevent him from trading and living a comfortable life.

As I get older, it becomes ever clearer to me that the best in the world finds its expression in simple human relationships: the love of a husband for his wife and parents for their children, the comradeship of men, compassion, patience and simple decency; while any ideology and doctrine, if not used with care as a working hypothesis, may lead to the chopping off of heads or, in the best of cases, to the stuffing of money bags.

The fact that two persons who were able to meet more than ten years ago without any interference and now, in the period of 'détente', are unable to meet does not speak in favour of détente's humanitarian aspects.

It does not seem to me correct, in light of the long-range problems of the US rather than the immediate ones, that there is a desire 'not to overload' détente, as Mr Kissinger has said, with humanitarian problems, and to yield on humanitarian issues as politically unimportant and annoying to the USSR all in order to promote the sale of Pepsi-Cola.

If the US sets itself the objective of establishing truly friendly relations with the USSR and wants to be assured of their durability, then it must strive for the transformation of the closed Soviet system to an open one. The awakening of the Soviet people to human rights is a force working in this direction.

Inasmuch as the movement for human rights has no troops, the politician–policemen and the politician–businessmen are inclined to slight it. But it seems to me that it is precisely the world movement for human rights that will become a world-transforming force that will overcome both inhumanity based on violence and inhumanity based on indifference.

Genuine stability comes only in a process of movement, only in the expansion of influence. The US must strive for a transformation of the world if it wants it to be more stable. A system that does nót set expansionist goals for itself contracts and dies away. The world has experienced many forms of expansion – military, economic and cultural. If the US can become the centre of a new expansion, a humanitarian expansion based on human rights throughout the world, its future would be assured for a long time.

It is interesting that this idealistic element has already, to a lesser or greater degree, been felt in American politics during the entire history of the US. The old-fashioned European political mentality – without an understanding of historical perspective and without interest in higher goals – is not likely to long dominate the foreign policy of the US. No matter how much more Mr Kissinger wants to cast aside humanitarian problems, they come to the surface by one means or another. This is particularly evident in the differences between the Administration and the Congress over the question of trade and of emigration from the USSR.

These differences, although restricting the Administration, also do give it certain benefits. The triangle of Mr Kissinger, Mr Brezhnev and Henry M. Jackson reminds me somewhat of the situation when a criminal is being induced to confess by two interrogators, one of whom – Senator Jackson – shouts and beats his fist on the table, and the other – Secretary of State Kissinger – who smiles and gently promises leniency. So the heart of the criminal, faced with such contrasts, opens up to the kind smile.

The US Government evidently is feeling the pressure of business circles, headed by makers of soft drinks, interested in cooperation with the USSR because they consider it a gigantic potential market for their products and a source of raw materials and cheap labour. One can only welcome economic cooperation if it is one of the elements of the policy of détente, but not a force shaping this policy.

Without doubt, businessmen have made an enormous contribution to the creation of modern America, but when they became the leading political force they led the US to the brink of disaster – to the Great Depression of the 1930s. It should come as no surprise that it is precisely the capitalists who are so boldly urging their government on to cooperation with those whose declared aim is their destruction. Over 100 years ago the English trade unionist Thomas Dunning wrote the following passage which Marx quotes with approval: 'When sufficient return is available capital grows bold. Guarantee it 10 per cent and capital is agreeable to any application; at 20 per cent it becomes excited, and at 50 per cent it is positively prepared to rack its brains . . .'

Americans are a people easily carried away. When they were carried away by the cold war, I don't know whether there were sober voices proposing some kind of alternative. Now the Americans are carried away by 'détente', and it is good that warning voices are being heard. The warning is that détente requires restraint and determination – not merely a willingness to compromise – and that meek concessions will only lead to demands for more concessions. Perhaps the voices will be heeded.

The alternative to détente, which its supporters have demanded to hear from its critics, is détente carried out differently, détente in which long range goals are not sacrificed to short-term goals; and one must learn to wait for what is desired.

Foreign policy does not exist by itself. It is an integral part of a country's internal condition, which in turn depends upon external conditions. If one accepts the premise that without *rapprochement* with the USSR the US cannot exert influence on it, then one must say that if this influence is not in a constructive direction the *rapprochement* will be even dangerous for the US. When the USSR must pay for every bushel of grain and for every technological secret not so much with gold as with a step towards democratization of its society, only then will its foreign policy cease to present a threat to the West.

However, this exchange, this 'gentle pressure' should not have the character of wounding the self-respect of the USSR. Let it proceed under the banner of demanding fulfilment from the USSR of the international declarations it has signed. And every concession should be looked upon not as a 'victory for the West' but rather as a step towards common good.

In the emerging triangle of powers, the relationship of the US towards the USSR and China, amid some similarities, is very different. China has not developed yet to the level of true partnership with the US economically, socially or politically; and militarily it presents much less of a danger to the US than does the USSR. Further, the mainspring of revolution still has not unwound in China. Any attempt to put pressure on China for the purpose of internal change most probably will yield no results. China is still so far from the West that everything that happens there is regarded almost like something on the moon. China is still too 'alien' for public opinion in the West to reach out a hand to those who are subjected to persecution.

It is a different matter with the USSR. From the circumstances of its tragic Eurasian geographic situation, Russia has always been both more sensitive to the West and more dangerous to the West than has China. The mainspring of the Russian Revolution has completely unwound. And moving now only by the force of inertia, the USSR will be highly responsive to pressure from the West, all the more so because of a hostile China at its back. And it is fully clear that the more the relations of the USSR with the West expand, the more it becomes 'familiar' to the West, the more public opinion in the West will keep an alert watch on events in the USSR.

If the rivalry of the USSR and China becomes ever sharper, and I believe that it will, then the ties of the US to the USSR and China will become like two sets of reins in the hands of the American leaders, which they can use to guide the course of world history.

But the question is, Will they?

Let us assume that a state or a group of states, working out long-range policies, should define the goals, strategy and tactics. As viewed from here in Russia, one might say that the political strategy of the US is correct, but that its tactics in effect are undermining that strategy. But what is more important, the policies of the US – and even more so of the West in general – reveal very dim objectives or even the absence of objectives; the preservation of the status quo and economic growth are not really objectives.

Perhaps the dissent and lack of confidence that have seized the West and have found partial reflection in 'détente' will open the way to a perception of the significant objectives – the objectives of reshaping the world, at the basis of which will be the human personality, a personality in its broad human, not egoistic, essence. Then the West, sure of itself, will begin to speak in a different voice.

One Year after Helsinki

As its title suggests, this article is an assessment of the effectiveness – or otherwise – of the Helsinki Agreements with regard to the Soviet Union. It was written in July 1976, just after Amalrik's arrival in the West. This translation first appeared in the Observer *on 8 August 1976. A French translation was published in* Le Monde *for 8/9 August 1976.*

When I now ask people in the West what has been achieved by signing the Helsinki Agreement, they reply that, first, the USSR promised not to touch West Berlin; and second, contact between the USSR and the West has been eased, and that this will lead to an improvement in the situation within the USSR. These arguments do not sound convincing to a man who arrived from Moscow only three weeks ago.

The USSR promised not to touch West Berlin as early as 1945, and there has been more than one 'Berlin crisis' since then. On each occasion the West made concessions to the USSR in return for preservation of the status quo, and the USSR reduced its pressure on Berlin for a period of several years. This has happened time and again, and gradually, over the years, the concept of the 'status quo' has changed, because all the concessions made by the West in previous years have been included in it. I do not rule out the possibility that the Berlin problem may arise again in five years' time, and that the West will again have to make some kind of concession to avoid a serious crisis.

As for the internal situation in the USSR, the easing of contacts and the greater freedom of information, success seems to me to be even more dubious. The authorities have, in fact, begun to be more careful in their treatment of well-known dissidents.

They did not, for example, put me in prison for seven years, as they did Sergei Kovalev.[1] Nor did they kill me at the door to my flat, as they killed Konstantin Bogatyrev.[2] Instead, by following me constantly, detaining me and threatening me with arrest and murder, they simply forced me to emigrate. Similarly, the authorities have refrained from arresting several other people, who earlier had been given clearly to understand that they would be arrested. But with people who are less well known, the authorities stand on as little ceremony as ever.

The practice of putting dissidents in psychiatric hospitals has decreased, but it has not ceased. Vladimir Bukovsky, who did more than anyone else to tell the West the truth about Soviet psychiatric hospitals is still serving the twelve-year sentence he was given for this.[3]

Another thing: as if to compensate for being unable to carry out massive 'legal' arrests under the new conditions, the KGB more and more often resorts to methods like murder, assault on the street, poisoning, arson and car accidents, while trying to make incidents like this serve as a 'warning' to others.

If there has been a change for the better, most of the credit for this is due to those Soviet dissidents who continually draw the attention both of the Soviet authorities and of the West to violations of human rights in the USSR.

In May of this year the Group to Monitor the Observance of the Helsinki Agreement (now known as 'the Moscow Helsinki Monitoring Group') was formed in Moscow, under the chairmanship of Professor Yury Orlov.[4] This group collects available information on any violation of the agreement in the USSR, and sends it to heads of all the Governments who signed the agreement. Although Professor Orlov was detained by the KGB on the day after the group was formed, and warned that he would be held responsible, the group has not disintegrated, and it continues its work.[5]

There is no evidence of any improvement in the dissemination of information. Indeed, one could talk about deterioration. As before, no Western newspapers are on open sale in the USSR, apart from Communist papers, and not all issues of these are available. Even the information carried by Soviet newspapers and journals about the West has been reduced in the last year. And as before, dissemination of *samizdat* is considered a criminal offence.

The jamming of radio broadcasts beamed at the USSR continues as it did before the signing of the Helsinki Agreement. The Voice of America, the BBC and the West German Deutsche Welle are not jammed openly, but in many areas there are Soviet broadcasts on the same wavelengths, and it is almost impossible to hear the foreign stations. Radio Liberty is constantly the main object of attack. Not only is it openly jammed (which is not very effective outside the large towns), but it is consistently attacked in the Soviet press.

At every personal meeting, Soviet officials tell the Americans that closing down Radio Liberty would represent a big step forward in the improvement of Soviet–American relations. Using their piecemeal tactics, the Soviet leaders would like to reach some compromise with the Americans and finish off Radio Liberty, pretending that they do not object to other Western stations. Then they would set to work against the Voice of America and other radio stations, and deprive millions of Soviet citizens of any non-Soviet information.

I am not sure that the position of Western journalists in Moscow has improved much in the last year. While they have been allowed to use multiple visas, and movement within the country has been slightly facilitated, their contacts with Soviet citizens are as hampered as ever. They even have to refer to the authorities for permission to interview anyone.

No Western journalists have been expelled from Moscow in the past year, but here, as with the dissidents, the authorities try to act more deviously. For example, they used the worldwide campaign against the CIA and announced, completely without foundation, that three American correspondents were on the CIA payroll. The 'guilt' of these journalists was that they wrote about things the Soviet authorities found unpleasant, particularly about the Movement for Human Rights. The Soviet authorities presented them as 'spies'; this was directed more at

Western readers than at Soviet ones – Western readers might at least partly believe it (after all, there is no smoke without fire), the three journalists would be morally compromised, and other journalists would think twice before writing anything objectionable.

Postal and telephone links between Soviet citizens and the West have become more difficult rather than easier. A vast number of letters and parcels do not reach their destinations, conversations are interrupted, and telephones are cut off for six months, for a year, sometimes for ever.

On exchange of information, the Soviet Press often points out that many more Western writers are translated into Russian and many more Western films are shown in the USSR than vice versa. This, of course, is not because of the ill-will of Western governments, but merely because Western culture is far richer than Soviet culture, and offers a wide choice. In any case, when the Soviet authorities complain about the paucity of translations, they exclude Solzhenitsyn, Brodsky, Sinyavsky, Voinovich, Kornilov, Maksimov, Gladilin, Gorbanevskaya, Erofeyev[6] and many others from Soviet literature – and these writers are all translated in the West. If Idi Amin had signed the Helsinki Agreement, he too would doubtless have complained that the West was offering more books and films than Uganda could offer in return.

Leaving the Soviet Union remains possible only for a few people, and it involves humiliating procedures. Even if one is only going to visit relatives for a while, one has to produce favourable references from one's place of work, signed by the director, the secretary of the party organization, and the chairman of the local trade union branch. Women are obliged to undergo a gynaecological examination before holidaying abroad.

Emigration has decreased in the last year, although thousands of people, mostly Jews and Germans, apply to leave. Those who apply are usually dismissed from their jobs and subjected to continual petty persecution. Sometimes they are even arrested – this discourages others from applying. The only concession to the

Helsinki Agreement had been a reduction in the price of an exit visa, from 400 to 300 roubles.

There is good reason for saying that the only positive result of the Helsinki Agreement has been the formation of the Helsinki Monitoring Group. The successful work of this group and its sympathizers could gradually force the USSR to fulfil the obligations it undertook. Therefore the attitudes of the Soviet authorities and of the West to this group will be an indication of how seriously each takes Helsinki. It is in the West's own interests to help the group, as well as the Movement for Human Rights in the USSR in their struggle to democratize the Soviet system and to turn it into a more open and less aggressive society.

The Soviet Union supports official contacts, sometimes very close, with Western governments, but it does not reject its friends in the West. For some reason the West, through many official and unofficial representatives, tries to ignore its friends in the USSR. The West accepts the rules of the game imposed by the Soviet Union. It looks on members of the Movement for Human Rights as if they were members of some dangerous underground movement, with whose 'romantic' aspirations it can sympathize from afar, but with whom it must avoid any personal contact. Yet the activities of the Movement are legal within the Constitution of the USSR.

The West fusses over the USSR continually, as over a spoiled child. It is afraid to 'offend' Soviet leaders even slightly, saying that they will 'become obstinate', 'become worse', and so on. Sometimes the West loses any kind of moral yardstick. How else can one explain the invitation to the ex-chief of the Soviet Secret Police to visit England as representative of Soviet workers?[7] Or the behaviour of Dr Leigh, the (then) Secretary-General of the World Psychiatric Association, who, while in the Soviet Union, fought shy of talking to General Grigorenko, a prisoner in a psychiatric hospital, and, at the same time, invited one of the psychiatrists who collaborate with the KGB to visit England, referring to him as a very amiable and obliging man?

Whether the West becomes socialist or remains capitalist, it will be able to keep its freedom and its 'human face' only if it retains its sense of dignity. And the dignity of the system as a whole, as well as of the individual, is best judged by its attitude to the strong and its attitude to the weak. At present we see how obliging the West is when dealing with the strong – with the Soviet Government; and how neglectful and distrusting it becomes with the weak – the Movement for Human Rights. This bodes ill for the West.

Within the terms of the Helsinki Agreement, what then do I think the West could do?

Western governments and Western public opinion should demand that the USSR cease jamming Western broadcasts. If sections of the Western public consider these broadcasts unsatisfactory, or think that they serve the 'cold war', then they can control the radio stations and change the content of the programmes. In my opinion, the closure of these stations, and particularly of Radio Liberty, which broadcasts exclusively to the USSR, would deliver a blow not only to the cold war, but also to millions of Soviet citizens who will then be deprived of any information apart from that given by the Soviet official press. At present, they at least have a chance to make comparisons.

Foreign governments should defend the rights of their citizens to take books published abroad into the USSR, including books by Soviet authors who live in the Soviet Union or who live abroad. If Members of Parliament and public leaders from abroad visiting the Soviet Union saw not only officials, but also independent Soviet public figures like Andrei Sakharov, winner of the Nobel Peace Prize, Professor Yury Orlov, chairman of the Moscow Helsinki Monitoring Group, and Valentin Turchin,[8] head of the Russian section of Amnesty International, it would be important.

It would also be important if foreign diplomats kept constant contact with representatives of the independent public, as well as with officials. Only under these conditions will they be able to furnish their governments with objective information about the situation in the USSR. On occasions like national holidays, foreign ambassadors could invite independent public figures as well. I have in mind particularly the Ambassadors of West Germany, Italy, Britain and France – great European powers. On 14 July the French Ambassador ought to invite several dissidents, as well as the several hundreds of official figures. This would be more in accord with the ideals of the French Revolution than the presence of the dozens of open and secret KGB agents who usually jostle one another at such receptions.

It would be a good thing if all the people who send letters to the USSR, or book telephone calls, tried to find out the reasons why letters do not arrive or telephone connections are not made, and then sent protests to the Soviet Embassy.

The information which reaches the West from the USSR, and which gets back from the West to the USSR, depends to a large extent on foreign correspondents in Moscow. If foreign journalists had their own club in Moscow, if they had a corporate feeling and enjoyed the support of their colleagues in the West, it would be helpful. On the whole Western journalists tend to be indifferent when one of their number struggles desperately with the Soviet regime for the right to send independent information to his readers. What is just as bad, they tend to be equally indifferent when one of their colleagues licks the behind of the Soviet authorities.

Europe and the Soviet Union

This article, written in September 1976, was published in English translation in Survey, No. 100/101, Summer/Autumn 1976, and is reproduced here by permission of the editor. The translator was Hilary Sternberg.

I have the impression that the prevailing opinion in the West is that there is no threat of a Soviet military invasion of Europe. I would myself be very surprised if Soviet troops were to cross the West German or Austrian frontier tomorrow. The Soviet Union appears to be more interested in preserving the status quo in Europe and in obtaining recognition of what it has already achieved than in launching a frontal attack. We may assume that Soviet expansion is more cautious and chooses more circuitous routes via Africa and the Middle East, while the troops stationed in Eastern Europe are more probably intended to lend weight to every word the Soviet Union directs at Western European governments. Those troops do not need to make any move; their presence alone and the aura of power emanating from them exert a considerable influence on the situation in Europe.

Yet I believe European security is based neither on the good-will of the Soviet Union nor on the will of the European states to resist – which is highly questionable – but on three precarious factors.

The first of these is the American military presence in Europe, which threatens the Soviet Union with a retaliatory nuclear strike and restrains the USSR from taking risky steps such as, for instance, the occupation of West Berlin.

Secondly, there are the USSR's own domestic difficulties and its attitude of mistrust towards the countries of Eastern Europe.

These problems impel the USSR into economic cooperation with the West and also prompt it to attempt to establish stable relations in Europe.

The third factor is the constant threat from China and the desirability of tranquillity in the rear in the event of an open Sino-Soviet confrontation.

If we assume that Western European security is indeed based on these three factors combined, we must consider it highly unstable.

In the first place, the American military presence cannot be regarded as permanent. Isolationist ideas may one day triumph in the USA, or there may even be a readiness to view the whole of Europe, not just its Eastern part, as the Soviet sphere of influence and as the price to pay for the USSR leaving the USA alone. The notion that the withdrawal of US troops from Western Europe in exchange for a partial Soviet troop withdrawal from Eastern Europe will lead to improved US–Soviet understanding and promote international stability may become very popular in the USA. The American public still does not understand the real nature of the Soviet Union and is prone to regard it as a superpower just like the USA, i.e. having foreign political ambitions, but striving towards a reasonable compromise. In fact, if a mutual troop withdrawal were to take place, the USSR, using its land frontiers, would easily be able to put them back at short notice, while the USA would find this extremely hard to do, both for strategic and political reasons.

In the second place, Soviet domestic problems such as the economic troubles, intensifying discord between nationalities, the conflict with the intelligentsia and other factors, may prompt the Soviet leaders to seek their solution precisely in foreign political conflicts, as Russian governments before them have tried to do, on the eve of the 1905 and 1917 revolutions. In addition, if no application is found for it abroad, the growing army will constitute a permanent threat to the Soviet political leadership.

Thirdly, the possibility always remains that the USSR and China will find a common language. This is especially likely now that, following the death of Mao Tse-tung, China might experience an internal political struggle and will endeavour not to exacerbate relations with its northern neighbour. It is, moreover, quite possible that victorious 'moderate' elements would try to establish neighbourly – if reserved – relations with the USSR and make the USSR feel that its rear is safe. In addition, it is said that pro-Soviet elements are still strong in the Chinese army. I do not believe that any good relations the USSR may establish with China will last for very long, and I consider a conflict between them sooner or later almost inevitable; but for a certain time they may have a mutual understanding and even reach agreement on the division of spheres of influence in Europe and Asia, and this may foreshadow hard times for Europe. Furthermore, European indifference to China, coupled with the ambiguous stance of the USA, which has clearly been trying to establish closer relations with the USSR, using China simply as a means of blackmail, may accelerate the process of Sino-Soviet *rapprochement*..

Unless the Western states – and in the first instance the USA – can summon up enough political will to withstand the USSR in Europe and try to influence Soviet internal liberalization, unless they have enough political wisdom to attempt a *rapprochement* with China, supporting its stand of independence from the USSR, France and Britain may one fine day find themselves in the position of Hungary or Czechoslovakia.

Détente and Democracy

The writing of this article spanned a whole year, from December 1975 to December 1976, during which its author emigrated from the Soviet Union. This translation is by Tobi Frankel and was published in Newsday *on 27 April 1977.*

> 'I will buy all!' said the gold
> 'I will take all!' said the sword.
>
> – Alexander Pushkin

Evidently, an intuitive understanding of a people's psychology means at least as much as if not more than a formal analysis of their political strengths. Failure to understand the psychology of the Vietnamese peasant has already led Americans into the foolish venture with the strategic settlements which clearly caused the defeat of the United States. Failure to understand the psychology of the Soviet leaders – and thus rushing into détente with the long-range goal of a Soviet–American diumvirate – may lead to even sorrier results.

Kissinger, the creator of this ambiguous form of détente, may have been an experienced strategist, but a strategist of retreat, and he came to personify the frustration that enveloped the United States as a result of the Vietnam war. But even if it is recognized that the retreat is temporary, it is the consequence of those back-breaking foreign political tasks which the United States set itself and on which it focused during the Vietnam war.

It seems to me that the basic mistake of the United States in the last thirty years has been that it has fought 'communism' geographically – if one can call it that – and not politically. Accepting 'communism' where it already existed, the United States in every possible way opposed its spread to new territories, supporting any frail regime as long as it was anti-communist, with little interest in the internal causes of communist revolution.

The United States was so little interested in the internal resistance to 'communism' where it held power, that Americans did not understand that the better way to overcome it was from the inside. Following the strange politics of encouraging 'communism' where people did not want it, and of opposing it where people wanted it, the United States not only lost in Vietnam, but also seemed absolutely unprepared for the events in Hungary in 1956 and in Czechoslovakia in 1968 or for the beginning of the Movement for Human Rights in the Soviet Union. The government of the United States saw them either as a hindrance to its own foreign policy or as politically insignificant phenomena.

We may now expect dramatic events in Poland. But the position of the Soviet Union seems to me by no means stable. The last seven years have underscored the tendencies I noted in my book, *Will the Soviet Union Survive Until 1984?*, that will lead to the disintegration of the Soviet system.

Formerly I believed that war with China would be a catalyst which would hasten these internal processes. Chinese military backwardness and the developing relative flexibility of the Soviet leadership in the last few years will delay disintegration significantly beyond 1984, but the threat is inevitable, unless new political ideas are brought forward and radical, not palliative, reforms are carried out.

The Soviet democratic opposition, even though still very weak, is not unimportant as a possible source of political alternatives. Despite the arrests and exiles, the Human Rights Movement has survived for ten years and has become a factor whose influence is seen particularly in such phenomena as détente and Eurocommunism. Not only is it producing a slow revolution in the minds of the Soviet people; it also serves the rest of the world as an index of the mood of a significant part of a silent Soviet society.

I understand that it is very hard for the United States to

131

achieve a balance between resistance to 'communism' and agreement with 'communism'; for, inevitably, it must choose the one or the other. I do not think that the choice for the United States is between reducing the danger of war by controlling the arms race with the Soviet Union and risking constant conflict by strengthening democracy in the Soviet Union. On the contrary, the danger of war will be avoided only by transforming the Soviet Union from a closed to an open system; until that happens, the United States, despite mutual restraint on the growth of weapons, will always be under the threat of surprise attack.

An open society makes the control of weapons possible and unprovoked aggression impossible. The study of history shows a direct connnection between totalitarianism and aggression; therefore, every limitation on domestic violence is a potential restraint on violence abroad. In the interest of its own long-term safety, the United States must support the struggle for the democratization of the Soviet Union.

American supporters of détente speak about the need to maintain good relations with the Soviet Union, to avoid increasing instability in the world, to avoid a nuclear war through arms limitation, to support the Soviet economy by way of payment in return for political restraint abroad by the Soviet Union – and they take it on faith that every attempt to pressure the Soviet Union reinforces its toughness, at home and abroad.

However, all this is by no means self-evident.

The cause of the danger of world disintegration seems to be that the problem of poor versus rich people within countries has evolved into one of poor versus rich countries. The Soviet Union unites within itself a highly developed and a weakly developed country, an economy desiring to orient itself to the West, but which constantly conflicts with an ideology that attempts to gear itself to the Third World. Therefore, the Soviet Union is always capable of unexpected and destructive steps, and all the benefits received from the United States can be directed to destruction of the world's stability. The latest example of this is Angola.

The world has preserved itself by maintaining a nuclear balance for three decades, as long as the risk of war has been too great. Were it not for nuclear arms, a war between the Soviet Union and the West would have started and ended long ago, only God knows how. In the framework of the nuclear balance, mutual arms reduction is undoubtedly better than their unchecked stockpiling, but I do not see how this by itself can prevent war; there are already enough nuclear arms to destroy the world several times over.

May I also recall that attempts to reduce armaments without proper controls, as happened between World War I and World War II, lead not to peace, but to mutual suspicion and the encouragement of aggression.

The contention that it is necessary to 'pay' the Soviet Union so that it will not increase disorder in the world makes an alarming impression. The idea of bribing the Soviet Union with the object of achieving détente and with economic help in particular – leads to political blackmail, to the Soviet Union demanding more and more in return for its own passivity. History is full of examples of 'trading' states paying off 'warlike' states, only to arouse their appetites, and I fear that in the final analysis no amount of American grain will alter the Soviet hard line.

It would have made great sense for the United States to conduct its economic policy with the Soviet Union only at governmental level, considering that the Soviet Union always wants to be the shark among the sardines and to deal with others individually, whether it be its own dissidents, European governments or American companies.

Unwillingness to 'pressure' the Soviet Union stems solely from fear of taking the smallest risk. To exert pressure is dangerous, but not to exert pressure is still more dangerous, because it means that the United States will itself become the target of increasing pressure. It seems to me that Americans must constantly ask themselves not only why the United States is interested in détente, but why the Soviet Union is interested in it; only after such analysis can it be decided how far the United States should go with its demands.

It is not a matter of constant pressure or constant concession, but rather that each of your actions should be appraised only in the light of your previous persistence.

It is inadmissible to conduct a policy of ultimatums with regard to the Soviet Union or to offend its pride, just as it is inadmissible that the Soviet Union should be allowed to offend the prestige of the United States. But the gradual mellowing of Soviet–American relations, in order to be real and not illusory, must be accompanied by a gradual mellowing of Soviet internal conditions.

As in every helping of a 'bloody Mary' there must be a dose of tomato juice, so in every 'helping' of détente there must be a dose of democratization of the Soviet system. Otherwise, the cocktail will gradually ruin the American stomach.

Are There Political Prisoners in the USSR?

The Soviet political journal Novoye Vremya (New Time), *in its No. 1, 1976, issue, published an interview with Soviet First Deputy Minister of Justice Alexander Sukharev. In what was clearly a carefully timed propaganda exercise (dissident biologist Sergei Kovalyov had three weeks earlier been sentenced to a total of ten years' imprisonment and exile on charges of anti-Soviet agitation and propaganda) Sukharev denied the existence of political persecution in the USSR and claimed that people like Kovalyov were only imprisoned for having committed specific illegal acts. He also insisted that the Soviet citizen's rights are fully guaranteed by the country's laws and constitution. Amalrik immediately responded with an article refuting Sukharev's claims. By now, having accumulated considerable experience of political imprisonment, he was living the uncomfortable life of the ex-prisoner, his movements monitored by the police and his choice of residence restricted.*

This translation is by Hilary Sternberg.

The interview granted by USSR First Deputy Minister of Justice Mr Alexander Sukharev to the journal *Novoye Vremya* (*New Time*), No. 1, 1976, merits a reply by someone who has had direct personal experience of the justice Mr Sukharev represents.

Having spent six years in prison, labour camp and exile, I read this interview with a mixture of delight and disgust. Delight, inasmuch as the very fact of this long-winded attempt (running to five pages in the journal) to justify Soviet penal policy indicates just how sensitive the Soviet government is to the reaction of world public opinion to violations of human rights in the

135

USSR and, consequently, just how much public opinion could achieve here. Disgust, because almost all of Mr Sukharev's assertions are lies, and lies are always unpleasant to read.

Mr Sukharev claims that from the very beginning 'Soviet law' has prosecuted only for 'specific actions' and not for a person's beliefs or for membership of a particular social group or party.

In reality, however, a system of hostages has existed from the very first months of the Bolshevik revolution, a system whereby certain people are held answerable for other people. In July 1918 Trotsky proposed that the wives and children of officers called up into the Red Army should be held as hostages in concentration camps. In August, calling for 'merciless terror', Lenin ordered: 'Dubious persons to be shut away in concentration camps.' In September the People's Commissar for Internal Affairs, Petrovsky, telegraphed local soviets: 'Take a considerable number of hostages ... from amongst the bourgeoisie and the officers.'

Similarly, it is well known – and from Soviet sources too – that hundreds of thousands of people were sent into exile or imprisoned in concentration camps between 1929 and 1931 not for any 'specific acts' but simply because they were so-called 'kulaks' and 'kulak sympathizers', that is, prosperous peasants and people who wished to live well. Their wives and children were deported with them.

Nor was it necessary to commit any 'specific acts' to become a victim of repressions in 1941–5: it was sufficient to be a Crimean Tatar, a Volga German, a Kalmyk, an Ingush or a Chechen.[1] It is well known that these and other national minorities were subjected to mass deportation.

Thus the operation of Soviet justice – if justice it can be called – was based initially on a class and then a racial approach and not at all on the concept of 'specific actions'.

Mr Sukharev repeatedly insists that no one has ever been tried for his political or religious convictions in the USSR and that he knows of no law enabling prosecution for one's convictions. Such a law does exist, in the shape of Article 70 (anti-Soviet agitation and propaganda) and Article 190–1 of the Criminal

Code of the Russian Federation (dissemination of information defamatory to the Soviet system), not to mention the use that may be made of other articles of the Code and even of extra-judicial confinement in psychiatric hospitals.

Soviet justice officials attach a specific meaning to the word 'belief'. I and other prisoners have been told on several occasions: 'You can hold whatever beliefs you wish, but you may not express them. We are not trying you for your beliefs but because you have expressed them.' Obviously it is impossible to try a man for a belief he has not expressed or made manifest in any way, since no one has yet invented a machine for reading people's thoughts. However, once an unorthodox thought has been ex-pressed, whether printed, written down or spoken, it is regarded as an indictable act. Furthermore, whether the idea that has been expressed is viewed as 'anti-Soviet' or not depends entirely on considerations of context and circumstance, for no legal definition of the concept 'anti-Soviet' exists.

To qualify as 'anti-Soviet', an utterance need not necessarily be a call for the violent overthrow of the Soviet system. All the instances I know of have concerned either criticism of specific aspects of that system or speculation as to possible directions in which it might evolve – and the criticism has frequently been from Marxist positions. Likewise, in the majority of cases where people have been tried and convicted, including my own case, the charge has not been one of having had connections with any 'centres abroad', and in instances where it has been, the ac-cusation has remained unproven.

People are tried not only for their own utterances or writings but also for reading or possessing books which the investigatory organs and the judge may deem 'anti-Soviet', although no pub-lished list exists of books which it is forbidden to possess or read.

It may well be that there are people in political camps who really have been convicted on account of 'specific acts' – Mr Sukharev mentions, in particular, persons convicted of wartime collaboration with the Germans. These people are often exploited in the camps by Mr Sukharev's colleagues for the purpose of harassing real political prisoners, while Mr Sukharev himself wants to use these pitiful characters to conceal thousands of people who fought against fascism or grew up after the war and dared to have their own opinions.

Just as false is the impression Mr Sukharev wishes to create of 'places of confinement'. In reality the 'food rations' he mentions are expressly intended to cause emaciation; food parcels up to five kilogrammes are allowed once every six months, after half the sentence has been completed; correspondence is restricted and many letters are confiscated or simply stolen by the camp administration; visits are allowed once every six months – and even this right may be withdrawn at the whim of the administration; the acquisition of literature is restricted – a prisoner is not permitted to have more than five books.

Beatings-up are not uncommon: I was kicked from one end of a railway carriage to the other during transportation from Sverdlovsk to Kamyshlov. After I had been ill with meningitis in prison I had my head beaten against a wall in my camp at Talaya and was dragged by the hair down from the third floor to the cellar of a prison in Magadan. On each occasion I lodged a complaint with the Ministry of Internal Affairs or the Procurator's Office – each time to no avail.

About the difficult situation of prisoners after their 'release' Mr Sukharev does not say a single word. Ex-prisoners are in fact considerably restricted in their choice of residence and work. Many of them who go to visit their families are tracked down and pursued by the police, for all the world like hunted animals. I myself have been hunted in this way: three times in three months I have been apprehended and threatened with re-arrest.

Finally, how is one to understand Mr Sukharev when he claims that 'since the war the conviction rate in our country has fallen by more than half'? Does he mean that in 1975 only half as many people were convicted as in 1945? Or that now there are only half as many people in prison as there were in the first post-war years? If so, it sounds rather odd.

After all, cautious estimates put the number of prisoners in our country at the end of the forties at about fifteen millions; after the war, trainload after trainload rolled East carrying ex prisoners-of-war, 'Vlasovites',[2] 'Bandera-ites',[3] ordinary convicts, political prisoners, collective farmers and enormous numbers of criminals and déclassés. Can it really be that now, after thirty years of relative well-being, after mass rehabilitations, the number of prisoners has dropped by only one half?

The total number of prisoners in our country is kept secret. According to my own rough calculation there are no less than three million of them – more than 1 per cent of the total population. However, in his eagerness to brag about the 'drop in convictions', Mr Sukharev paints a somewhat gloomier picture of a total approaching seven or eight millions.

Comparing my own impressions of prison in 1965 and in 1970–73, I would say that the number of prisoners has increased rather than decreased over that period of time. Although new blocks had been or were being built at almost all the prisons I saw the inside of – in Moscow, Sverdlovsk, Novosibirsk, Irkutsk, Khabarovsk and Magadan – the cells were overcrowded, sometimes with thirty men to a room meant for ten; in transit, fifteen or twenty men would be crammed into a train compartment for seven. While I was in the Magadan region, which has a population of 400,000 and where the only prisoners now serving their sentences there are local inhabitants, yet another camp was built to supplement the existing two prisons and five camps.

The situation of political prisoners is tragic. They belong to the most sensitive and the most right-thinking section of our people and at the same time to the exhausted and embittered many-million-strong mass of common prisoners, many of whom incidentally, are also innocent people who have been wrongly convicted. I hope Mr Sukharev, and his colleagues responsible for depriving them of their freedom, will not succeed in discrediting them into the bargain in the eyes of those who might have the power to help them.

January 1976
Moscow

Who are the KGB?

This short essay on the psychological make-up of the Soviet security police is dated 5 December 1976. It was published in English translation in the Far Eastern Economic Review *on 31 December 1976, and is reprinted here in a slightly expanded version.*

In the early 1950s, a man in his forties went to the local KGB headquarters in a small Siberian town (this was in the days when the KGB was still called the MGB[1]) and said he wanted to be put in jail. He hated the existing order and could not breathe the air around him, he said, and he could no longer put up hypocritical pretences.

Alarmed, the secret police agents did what they could to pacify him. 'Why look on the black side so much?' they said, 'After all, the dark sides are not the only ones to our life. And what makes you think we ought to put you inside? We're fighting the enemy, but you are just muddle-headed. Calm down, go home, do your job, and stop looking at life so one-sidedly. You'll soon see that everything's not that bad. And one day you'll come back here to thank us.'

A few months passed. The man was left alone, and he began to calm down. In actual fact something had snapped in him since his outburst, and life in the Soviet Union no longer seemed so bad. After six months, he dropped in on the KGB again and said: 'Comrades, you were right, I thank you!' They clapped him on the shoulder in a friendly way – and that night he was arrested on a charge of 'anti-Soviet agitation'.

This incident tells a lot about the *gebists* (a slang word for a KGB agent – derived from the Russian pronunciation of the letters *g* and *b*). Marxism – at any rate its Soviet version – has become a terrestrial religion, and the KGB a kind of monastic order. For a long time it bred up out of the mass of Soviet government servants those who were, on the one hand, the most fanatical, and on the other, the most cynical and hypocritical. Several times in its history this order was drastically reformed. At the start, the generation which was doomed to fail was physically annihilated. Later, people were just transferred to other work or pensioned off. But the essential nature of the order has never changed.

To gain a better insight into the psychology of people who work for the KGB – they always designate themselves by the vague word 'employees' – it is necessary to investigate how and from where they were assembled. The foundations were laid by the underground agents of the Bolsheviks and those who fought against them before the Revolution – the ranks of the Tsarist political police, the Okhrana. The latter, however, were employed (by the Bolsheviks) in secondary roles, somewhat in the nature of specialist engineers with 'red managers'. Dzerzhinsky[2] knew the importance of specialists.

The Party wanted to control its police, and the 'organs' were swelled constantly with party functionaries. The organs is a title which they gave themselves – an abbreviation of the phrase 'organs of state security'. During my childhood, the word 'organs' induced terror. Now it seems more comic than terrible, because of its association with sexual organs. The younger generation of *gebists* talk about 'the committee'.

As for Party control, this has not always been successful. There was a time when the organs controlled the Party, rather than the other way round. Even now, Party functionaries who have taken on jobs in the organs take on a particular air. The country has always been covered by a gigantic net of part-time informers. Some work out of conviction; others for the sake of small benefits or the possibility of evening scores with someone; still others from fear. Those who prove themselves best are transferred to permanent employment.

The Komsomol (Communist Youth League), and in particular

at the level of its highest functionaries, is one of the KGB's main suppliers. This is how the system works at present. When a responsible Komsomol worker reaches a particular age – it seems to be thirty-five since the Komsomol is a youth organization – he is transferred to other work. Those who have distinguished themselves most go into the Party apparatus; the dull-witted and stubborn go into the trade unions and the Ministry of Culture; the 'golden mean' types go into the KGB.

In so far as the KGB wants to extend its influence everywhere, it desires and is able to breed people to work for it wherever it wants. The KGB has links with the ordinary police force: it entices policemen who catch its eye. It keeps an eye on those who are serving temporarily in military commands assigned to itself and to the Ministry of Internal Affairs, and offers them a chance to 'rise'. It likes to take on former sportsmen, and it seeks out specialists in different fields – biologists, mathematicians, linguists, electrical engineers. Under the supervision of one such engineer – a rather likeable young man – when I was exiled in Kolyma, I used to take trips to view the construction of the Kolyma hydroelectric plant. He used to tell me how mighty Soviet power was, since it could build hydroelectric stations even so far north, and he used to enjoy beating me at chess. Before we parted, he asked me with a faintly timid air for an autographed photo.

In the end – for such is human nature – KGB agents try to recruit people from their own circle: children, brothers and sisters, distant relatives, close acquaintances, and people with whom they feel an instinctive affinity. All these currents pass through various kinds of special training centres and are saturated with a strong spirit of caste.

Just as the heart draws blood to itself, and at the same time disperses it around the whole body, the KGB – the heart of the Soviet system – draws employees from everywhere and pushes them out again everywhere – into trading concerns, the press and the diplomatic service, with the idea that they should spread out not just over the whole country, but over the whole world.

This penetration of and contact with real life makes the *gebists* much better informed and more pragmatic than, say, Soviet ideologues. For the past twenty years – to the extent that the KGB's role in the system has been reduced – there has been a noticeable transformation of *gebists* from fanatics, or people pretending to be fanatics, into ordinary officials fulfilling their duties more or less indifferently.

But the caste-like seclusion from society is powerful. It breeds not only a sense of one's own superiority, but also a more subconscious feeling of alienation and resentment. I have never met people more touchy than *gebists*. Any form of mockery can drive them wild. With some, the affected politeness falls away at the drop of a hat. Some try to smile, but it is obvious how much they are suffering inside. Not everyone, of course – scarcely anyone, in fact – makes fun of the employees of the organs.

It could be said that people hungry for power go into KGB work voluntarily as a form of compensation for their own insignificance. They are often people afflicted since childhood with an incapacity for study, or with characteristic cowardice, sadism, or other undesirable traits.

Like all Soviet people, in their heart of hearts they admire the West. Once a *gebist* said to me in tones of wonderment:

'Just imagine it – in America a policeman is a respected member of society and lots of women would gladly be married to him. But in our country what woman in her right mind would go for a policeman?'

You can see their weaknesses, but you will not always succeed in playing on them. First and foremost, because you never have dealings with any one of them as an autonomous human being; you are dealing with a huge machine, and each *gebist* is only a little wheel linked to other little wheels. On their own, they could not move by one millimetre, in case the machine fell apart.

Conversely, they try in every way to play on your weaknesses. They are not really such subtle psychologists, and they seek in a person some obvious and – to them – comprehensible weakness as a general means of pressure – fear, jealousy, envy, avarice, lust (for men or women), vodka, drugs. Their reliance on the worst and the most primitive implies that they themselves are neither complex nor good individuals. I recall that in order to trick them I had to make myself out much worse than I really am – and in an almost childish manner they unburdened themselves to me in return.

I remember how the head of the Magadan KGB headquarters used to try to persuade me to emigrate from the Soviet Union. They were so keen for me to leave that they even promised to cut four months off my sentence of exile. 'Why waste yourself here, Andrei Alexeievich,' he would say, smiling. 'Go to the West. That will be the life for you. You can buy yourself two cars, and visit night-spots.'

Often I saw him distressed, especially when he was talking about the cunning of the American imperialists and Japanese fishermen – the fishermen were annoying him in the Sea of Ok-hotsk – but then his face would light up as though from within. It was obvious that two cars and a night-spot were his own dream. Well, I have been half a year in the West, and to my shame I haven't bought one car yet, or even visited a night-spot. I don't think the fee for an article about the KGB will be enough for me to buy the car, so feel all the more called upon to spend it drinking in a night-spot.

An Involuntary Journey to Kaluga

In recent years the Soviet authorities have arrested dissidents and potential 'political troublemakers' on the eve of important events such as party congresses, visits by foreign statesmen or simply on major public holidays, and detained them for the duration of the occasion on some false pretext, e.g. for allegedly violating residence regulations. This happened to Andrei Amalrik on the weekend before the Twenty-fifth Congress of the Soviet Communist Party was due to commence in February 1976, and he afterwards took the opportunity to describe the extraordinary lengths to which the police went to prevent him from going about his business. The title of his narrative, suggested during the 'journey' by the KGB themselves by way of a joke, is, of course, a play on the title of An Involuntary Journey to Siberia. *The two journeys may have differed vastly in scale but their purpose was essentially one – to silence an unwelcome critic.*

The article is dated 25 February–1 March 1976. This translation, by Thompson Bradley, was published in Harpers, *August 1976, and is reprinted by permission of the Alexander Herzen Foundation, Amsterdam.*

The Twenty-fifth Party Congress was scheduled to begin on the morning of 24 February 1976. On the evening of Friday the 20th my wife, Gyuzel, and I were invited to the apartment of our friend, an American diplomat. We had asked him to meet us on the street outside. Quite often the policeman standing at the entrance gate would stop guests by demanding, 'Where are you going? What's the purpose of your visit? Show me your passport!'

Besides the gate guard, a lieutenant colonel and a major of the police, both in full uniform, were standing at the entrance, and that made me feel a bit uneasy. They looked at us intently without a word. Possibly, I thought, these were increased security measures on the eve of the party congress, yet a nagging sense of misgiving stayed with me.

When around 1.00 a.m. we left with our friends, Ina and Vitaly Rubin, there was no one standing at the entrance. The side street was empty. Somehow two men suddenly appeared about twenty yards behind us. After coming out into Lenin Prospect, we said good night to the Rubins and walked a short way to a cab rank. Almost immediately a car pulled up alongside us and out jumped the same two men. With the words 'Here, in here, Andrei Alexeievich!' they grabbed me. Struggling with them, I said, 'I'll get in, but first let me see your identification!' When they had shoved me half-way into the automobile – a third party was helping from inside – one of them, corpulent, with a sagging, drawn face, evidently the one in charge, showed me his red identification book, only, however, after covering his name and that of the institution which had issued it. Inasmuch as some form had been observed, I got into the car without any further resistance. Completely taken aback, Gyuzel managed only to cry, 'Where are you taking him?' and we were off.

'That's more like it, you should have done that from the start, Andrei Alexeievich,' the principal agent said, 'after all, it's not the first time.' All the while he kept glancing nervously around. His failure to show me his identification was reassuring; it meant that they were afraid of me. The affair was more like a kidnapping than a lawful arrest.

Saggy face kept on puffing and fidgeting nervously, unable to regain his composure after the heated struggle.

'Why are you so nervous?' I asked. 'After all, you're the authorities, you've got the power. What have you got to worry about?'

In an offended tone, he answered, 'We're flesh and blood, too. We're not made of steel.'

I must say that throughout this whole affair I generally kept my head better than did my abductors and those with whom I had to deal later on. I do not attribute that to bravery or self-control on my part and I do not want to say that I wasn't afraid, but it really was familiar to me. It was not the first time; I had gone through it all more than once, and this form of routine kept me fairly calm.

I guessed that the Rubins had not caught the trolley and that Gyuzel was with them. And that is how it turned out. Hardly had we reached the fifth district police station on Arbat Street when I heard the voices of Gyuzel and Vitaly through the window. The duty area, where they had settled in to wait for me, was located to the right of the entrance, and the room I was in to the right of that. Evidently it served as a classroom for police instruction. The walls were hung with diagrams of automatic weapons and excerpts from orders and instructions.

Here I spent two hours. I was guarded, first by two men and then by one fellow, still quite young and completely indifferent. He offered me a copy of *Vecherniaia Moskva*,[1] and I began to do the crossword. As it happened, my captors were also doing it and even asked me for a word here and there. To my shame I have to admit that our abilities turned out to be roughly equal. I, just like them, stumbled on a tragedy of Euripides'; they for some reason thought I knew all about Euripides' tragedies. Several times they took my passport from me and returned it right away. Bored with waiting around, I lay down on the bench and dozed off for a while.

Then the door to my room opened and in walked Major Kiselev. He happened to be the officer on duty in the station. In fact, I had already caught a glimpse of him. In a hurt tone he started up. How come I didn't greet him and didn't recognize 'old friends'? I was already tired and not in the mood for chatting. But when Kiselev mentioned my father, I cut him off, saying it was people like him who had driven my father to his death.[2] Kiselev became even more offended. He told me how he had aged (indeed, his appearance was quite flaccid and grey), yet he still did not want to retire.

'What?' I said, 'You mean you like your stinking work?'

'Someone has to work here,' Kiselev said angrily. He left and didn't come by again.

He took his anger out on the Rubins and Gyuzel, and he was

not very pleasant to my kidnappers, either. As it was related to me subsequently, he kept shouting at them through the glass partition, 'I have nothing to do with this! It's your affair! I'm not getting mixed up in it! He's well known! As it is, I've let you have a room; now you work it all out yourselves!'

They fussed about and spoke on the telephone to somewhere. One of them sat down near my wife and our friends, and was all ears. Two more agents arrived and talked on the phone for a long time. I lay on the bench and dozed in my room at the other end of the corridor.

'Get up, Andrei Alexeievich. Let's go,' said the one I took to be the chief. We went outside and got into the same car, the young fellow next to the driver and I in the back with my captors on either side. They were quite hefty, but on getting in they grumbled at me for taking up a lot of room.

Where I was being taken, I did not ask, as I did not ask about the reasons for my detention. We turned towards the centre of Moscow, and I thought, Not to the Lubyanka by any chance?[3] But along Marx Prospect we took a right turn in the direction of Kamennyi, and I wondered, To Lefortovo? But we drove on out to the Warsaw Highway. Nobody spoke. One of them kept glancing back to see whether any cars were following us.

Suddenly, the one on my left, about fifty, flabby, and unhealthy colouring to his face (one might say almost their common symptom), and with a foul smell emanating from his mouth, turned and asked, 'What's your name?'

'You mean you've arrested me and you don't know my name?' I said.

'Amalrik, Andrei Alexeievich,' he said, scowling, and added with sudden malevolence, 'Where do you work?'

'What's this?' I asked. 'You were speaking with me formally and suddenly you're right into the intimate —'

'You don't like that?'

'I have heard so much of everything from your kind already that on the whole I don't care,' I said. 'But if you want to talk with me you'd better be polite, and you might just identify yourself, too. Who are you?'

'Chernov, an employee of the Criminal Investigation Department,' said the latter, enveloping me with his vile breath. (It is interesting to note here that operatives of the KGB continually pass themselves off as CID employees. I remember as far back as 1962 how they seized me at night in a similar manner, even presented CID identification and took me off to the Lubyanka, where the agent in charge said to me proudly, 'Now, you see who we really are!'

'Why do you behave so insolently?' continued the man on my left.

'Have I offended you in some way?'

'Not me, but you have offended our society with your slander!'

'And are you,' I asked politely, 'speaking now on behalf of society, as it were?'

'Yes, on behalf of society.'

The man on my right said amiably, 'You, I see, view this with suspicion, Andrei Alexeievich, as you do everything else.'

For several kilometres we said nothing else. Once again, 'Chernov' started up: Now you don't work anywhere; your work is the spreading of slander. 'We know all about how you claim to be a historian, you see, how you give all kinds of hostile interviews and not a word of truth in them! Who called on your wife and proposed she get a divorce? You write every kind of slander!'

I answered that he was apparently confusing me with someone else, as I had neither said nor written anything about people suggesting to my wife that she divorce me. I guessed later that he seemed to have had in mind my letter to President Ford. I wrote there that the Soviet authorities refuse to consider invitations from foreign universities to Soviet citizens, mentioning also that I could not accept such an invitation since my wife had been refused an exit visa, and I was afraid to leave without her. There have been many well-known instances in which the Soviet government has not permitted wives to join their husbands or husbands to return to their wives.

Meanwhile, 'Chernov' kept muttering that they knew all about my interviews, that they also had my article on political prisoners[4] in their possession, and that they were just waiting for certain additional materials from abroad in order to hang a proper prison sentence on me. I kept quiet. All these conversations – and they all are tiresomely alike – had long ago become familiar to me. So boring was it all that I was not even interested enough to say something offensive to him. I kept quiet, which most likely irritated him even more.

As we approached the Moscow city outer limits, a traffic policeman waved for us to stop, but my abductors only grinned – and the policeman, realizing something was afoot, jumped back off the road.

'We're going to your birthplace,' said my right side.

'Well, since I was born in Moscow, it looks more as if we're leaving, but then all around here is my native land.'

'If you actually have one,' said my left side.

At this point it was discovered that we were travelling in the wrong direction; the driver didn't know the way. We came out on to the ring road and, after several kilometres, again headed away from Moscow, this time by way of the Kaluga Highway.

'Now Andrei Alexeievich can write *Involuntary Journey to Kaluga*' – the agent on my left still could not settle down. 'You see, we know about your *Involuntary Journey to Siberia*.'[6]

Although the bleakest thoughts had crossed my mind, I now considered much more probable two alternatives: either I was being taken to Vorsino, the village where I was registered and had a room, and would be under house arrest there until the end of the party congress, as was done with Ina Rubin during Nixon's visit, or I was being driven to Borovsk, the district centre, where I would be held in a preliminary detention cell on some trumped-up charge until the congress was over, as had happened to Vitaly Rubin, also during Nixon's stay. Nixon himself, as far as I know, was against the preventive arrest of Jews in connection with his visit.

The 'representative of Soviet society' finally shut up and leaned against me, his elbow painfully jammed into my side. I waited until he raised his arm to light a cigarette and managed to shift around and rest my elbow on him. It was stuffy and very cramped. Meanwhile, my speculations were not confirmed: we passed the turn for Vorsino, and then the exit for Borovsk.[6]

After two and a half hours we entered the suburbs of Kaluga.[7] Small wooden houses flashed by along the sides of the road. The man on my left started up again: slander, interviews, we're gathering material, the fate of Kovalev awaits you, I guarantee you that, a third prison term, you'll be put on special regime, we've had enough of this talking nice with you. He had spoken so convincingly that I was already sure that they actually had brought me to Kaluga for a third term. Why else, indeed, would they bring me here? I thought. Whether he was saying this on his own initiative or had instructions to frighten me along the way, I do not know. If he had been picked specially for this, then he was a good choice because the vile stench that issued from him with every word heightened the effect.

Once again the driver got lost and with difficulty found the main street. My right side said: 'Kaluga has a good space museum, and now Andrei Alexeievich will have a chance to see it.'

'How, I ask you, might I see it,' I said, 'when, according to citizen Chernov, I will be in prison on special regime?'

At this point we pulled up to the main administration building of the Ministry of Internal Affairs.[8]

'Go easy on yourself, at least, Andrei Alexeievich,' said my right side, as he got out. He said it in a tone which implied, 'You have no pity on us and make us work nights. At least go easy on yourself.'

In the hall of the Ministry of Internal Affairs building I spent ten or so minutes, then returned to the car again, and finally was delivered to the district police station on the outskirts of Kaluga.

'Take out your belongings, your money!' said the duty officer by way of greeting. My kidnappers stood nonchalantly in the doorway.

'I would like to know what I have been picked up for and why I have been brought here,' I said, as I unbuttoned my jacket and took out my wallet.

'How should I know?' replied the lieutenant. 'The chief will be in tomorrow; ask him.'

Just as indifferently I was searched (my wallet, notebook, glasses, watch, scarf and change purse were taken away) and led to the toilet, and with the same indifference did the sergeant throw open the cell door.

Some fifteen people, for the most part drunk, were seated or lay on the filthy floor. It seemed there was not even room to put your foot down. The stench was unbearable, and, to make matters worse, someone had already urinated in the corner. Through the screened, paneless window which opened not on to the outside street, but into the duty officer's room, we got very little air. On the other side of it I saw my abductors animatedly set to gutting my notebook. I was surprised they had not made me sign some kind of charge sheet or even an inventory of the belongings they had confiscated.

With difficulty I pushed aside two fellows who were asleep, spread out my jacket, and lay down on the floor. One of my cellmates had been left his watch: it was six in the morning. He said the chief would be there around ten.

I lay there with my eyes closed, but could not fall asleep. Before me was some grotesque mug, bristly, wrinkled, dirty, all bruised and bloody, and reeking of alcohol. Someone swore obscenely, meaninglessly another cried out in his sleep and waved his arms.

Towards eight o'clock everyone began to wake up and sprawl out on the narrow benches along the walls. Only one, with a swollen face and without coat or hat, continued to lie on the floor. He'd landed in there because in his drunken stupor he'd tried to take someone else's coat. It was quite cold outside and what he'd done with his own coat I do not know.

The news that I had been brought there from Moscow was received without interest. Everyone sat gloomy, hung over, awaiting judgement and punishment. Many were in for fighting, and some had been jailed by their wives. Others were simply drunkards. One, to my amazement, drank his own urine on the spot, so as not to smell of alcohol. This met with general approval. For almost all of them this was not the first time. They asked the duty sergeant for permission to go to the toilet and requested that the door be opened – we couldn't breathe. He responded lazily and called them out one by one to sign their charge sheets.

One fellow alone was in good spirits, a thief around thirty who was full of jokes and wisecracks. I caught sight of him a few hours later, though, really down in the dumps. He had been charged with robbery and was being transferred to prison. It was his second term.

My attention was also caught by a man of respectable appearance. It seemed he had been divorced from his wife, received a new apartment, and returned to his old place to collect his furniture. Drunk, he did not deny himself the pleasure of smashing up the furniture, and in the process his ex-wife had come in for some punishment, too, I think. That morning he was really cut up about it and spoke of how these days women were so liberated you couldn't say a word to them.

Actually, a strange breed of family has come into being in our country. All sorts of family difficulties are resolved exclusively with the help of the police, and at a somewhat higher level with the assistance of the union or party organization. Wives are continually calling in the police; husbands are put away for a fortnight or for several years and then return to those same wives. And the husbands are no better than their wives when it comes to calling the police and putting each other in jail.

At half past nine the deputy chief of the department – a major, it was said – arrived in civilian clothes and the trial began. People were summoned from the cell one at a time. The major, sitting at a table, would yell, 'How much longer must I mess around with you, you wretches! You're spoiling your own life and everyone else's! How long since you've worked? Why do you drink? Why did you have to piss on the street? And what makes you so free with your fists?'

In reply the accused, standing before the major, would mumble something or other. All of them explained that they weren't guilty of anything. The verdicts were speedily reached:

for this one a 30-ruble fine, that one to court to receive fifteen days, and this one to the examining magistrate for criminal proceedings. Only one, after being reprimanded, was freed.

I heard someone mention my name to the major.

'That one I won't even look at,' the major said and left.

Gradually people were led out of the cell – some to await trial until Monday, others to the examining magistrate. Around noon, when the lieutenant came in for someone else, I told him that I had been sitting there since the night before and no one had explained what I was being held for, why I had been brought there, or what they planned to do with me.

'You don't work!' he answered.

'Even if I don't work, that is not grounds for arresting me and bringing me here. After all, I have nothing to do with you.'

'You do!' the lieutenant said and slammed the door.

Several more hours passed. Meanwhile a man was brought in who was obviously insane, babbling a steady, loud stream of nonsense. In 1965, immediately after my trial, I spent several hours in a cell with an insane man like this one. So excruciating had that been for me that I thought I too would lose my mind. But by this time I had become accustomed to such things; I scarcely even took any notice of this fellow. I was transferred to an adjacent cell, alone, but then two drunk women were hauled in, and I was returned to the general cell. The two women began screaming at each other.

'You're a bitch,' cried one. 'I may not be much, but I work and am of use to society. What do you do?'

'I'm a prostitute!' yelled the other, though not so confidently.

Around three o'clock the lieutenant suggested that since I had money someone could be sent out to buy me something to eat.

'It's all right to send out,' I said, 'but you're in fact obliged to feed me by law.'

'Actually not, we have nothing to do with you,' the lieutenant said.

They bought me two bottles of kefir[9] and some rolls. I also asked them to return my glasses, and they did so then and there. Generally speaking, they became more and more obliging

155

towards me. I drank a bottle of kefir and walked about my cell, now in solitude. They had released the madman to avoid having to deal with him.

At this point a new person, just picked up, was led into the duty room. Drunk and with blood smeared all over his face, he thickly urged the lieutenant to take 20 rubles for himself and leave him just enough money for a cab so he might reach his dearly loved children. He had two briefcases with him. They opened one up – there proved to be only a woman's purse in it. They started opening the second, but what was in it I never found out: two young men in street clothes entered the duty room, and I was immediately brought out of my cell.

The young men greeted me, politely but with reserve. My belongings were collected by them. I acknowledged in writing that food had been procured for me at a cost of 1 ruble and 8 kopeks, and we left.

Outside there waited a green vehicle like a military jeep without any kind of police markings on it, yet behind the wheel sat a policeman. Once more we drove through the centre of town, past the buildings of the Ministry of Internal Affairs and Security Police and out on to a highway leading to Moscow. It was 4.00 p.m. on Saturday 21 February.

'Do you know where we're going?' said the young man in the front seat.

'No,' I said. 'I usually don't ask where I'm being taken since no one answers me anyway.'

'We're going to Borovsk.'

'What for?' I asked.

'When we arrive, you'll be told about that.' Having once again proved that one need not bother asking questions about anything, he retreated into silence.

The first lieutenant on duty at the Borovsk district police station met us with a big smile.

'We've met, we're already acquainted,' he said to my civilian travelling companions. 'And it seems you and I have met.' He turned to me, smiling. He probably had remembered me from the time when I had gone there to register.

I was led into a small passage behind the duty room; on to it opened the doors of the detention cells, and I could hear the lively voices and the laughter of prisoners. The sergeant-major shouted encouragingly from the corridor: 'Tea's coming soon, boys!' The situation here had a rather patriarchal character to it, and I thought that for me it would be better to do fifteen days with these 'boys' than in Kaluga.

I waited ten minutes or so. 'This way please,' said the duty officer, and we went upstairs to the office of the deputy chief, a young major with dark hair and a good-natured face. When we entered, he was sitting at his desk. To his right with a morose look sat the public prosecutor in the uniform of a judicial counsellor, an exact replica of those district prosecutors whom I had met so often earlier. And to one side sat the young man in civilian clothes who had brought me here. He had given his name as Surin.

I greeted everyone and took a seat next to the desk, and with that the major said: 'Have a seat.'

Straight away he started reproaching me; they had been sending summonses to me for four months and I had not shown up in response to them, so they had been forced to pick me up.

I said that if they had been sending me a summons it had been only very recently, since during the past four months not a single summons from them had come to me in Vorsino or to my wife's address in Moscow.

'Your wife is no concern of ours. We would not send anything for you to her,' the prosecutor said.

'At your place you will find a summons for 26 February,' the major remarked. 'You need not appear for it now since we were summoning you for this discussion.'

As it turned out, that police summons – the only one for the entire period of my registration there – had actually come to Vorsino and, contrary to what the prosecutor had said, to my wife's address in Moscow. The summons had been mailed from Borovsk on the evening of 19 February, and had reached Vorsino on the 21st and Moscow on the 22nd. In it I was invited to the district office of the police on 26 February 'with regard to matters pertaining to registration.'[10] Thus, because I had not appeared in Borovsk on 26 February in response to that summons, I was arrested in Moscow late at night between 20 and early 21 February. All the laws of time and space had been defied, yet that seemed to surprise no one.

And furthermore there was a little bit of deception in the summons itself – I had not been summoned concerning questions about my registration.

'Where are you working?' inquired the prosecutor. I had not succeeded even in opening my mouth when he repeated, 'Where are you working? Why are you registered in the Borovsk district?'

In reply I said that I had registered there, and had done so with great difficulty, not because I wanted to live and work there, but because I was not permitted to live in Moscow with my wife. I said that I found it absurd in the extreme that a man could be denied permission to live with his wife.

The prosecutor launched into a detailed retort – that many people were registered in this way with them and lived and worked here until their record of conviction had been removed and then they could return to their wives,[11] but then he sensed that this was diverting him from the main topic and again insistently repeated several times:

'Where do you work? Where do you work? We have a principle in this country: he who does not work, does not eat!'

'Oh, yes. The very words of Paul the Apostle,' I said. By then I had pretty much cheered up, for when I had been brought to Borovsk, I knew that my worst fears had not been realized.

My remark about Paul the Apostle annoyed the prosecutor greatly. 'Hold on, why are you giving us this business of Paul the Apostle? We know all that better than you do. Where do you work?'

'Here you are all excited, pressing so hard, not letting me get a word in edgewise,' I said, 'and look at me. I've just been through such a mess of trouble, and look – I simply radiate good cheer.'

At this I smiled as broadly as possible, radiating this good cheer. I wanted to add that, furthermore, amongst the people there had already arisen a saying 'as cheerful as Amalrik', but that seemed superfluous. The prosecutor settled down somewhat and the conversation continued more calmly.

The major joined in: I had been registered in their district for more than four months, and they had not bothered me all that time, but now they wanted to find out how I was and where I was working.

I replied, in the words of Yuri Maltsev, that I worked at my desk. I told them that I was a writer and that was my work and I did not see any need to take up any other and that I belonged to a writers' organization – I was a corresponding member of the Dutch section of the PEN Club.

'But that PEN Club is in Holland,' the prosecutor said, 'and we need to have you working in the territory of the Borovsk district.'

I replied that there were certain circumstances still to be considered. My wife and I had applied for temporary visas to go abroad, and until a decision had been made on that matter it made no sense to take a job anywhere; in fact, in our country, people lose their jobs for applying to leave the country. And it was not out of the question, either, after the kind of treatment I had received in the past twenty-four hours, that we might request a permanent exit visa from the USSR. In conclusion, I said that I was not in good health, and because of the after-effects of the suppurative meningo-encephalitis which I had had in prison I tired very easily. In prison I had been assigned to the second category of disability, and I could not do any kind of hard labour.

The prosecutor and the major made their objections to me in the course of the conversation roughly in the vein that, since I was not yet abroad, I might find myself a job now, one that was not too difficult. For the present, they said they were simply talking to me, although they might issue a formal warning. They advised me to go to Moscow and consult with my wife about finding myself a job. The prosecutor personally invited me to come to see him for a chat on Friday 27 February, as he also wanted to help me get a job.

I would drop by to see the prosecutor and gladly have a talk with him, I said, but regarding the formal warning, so far as I had heard, the USSR was a signatory to the international convention for the abolition of forced labour.

'It was not for your sake we signed it,' the prosecutor said.

The prosecutor departed, and the major then began trying to foist some form on to me to provide a written explanation of where I lived and why I had no job. I had no intention of writing anything of the sort. At first I spoke calmly about how the prosecutor had ordered me to consult with my wife first and how I was the kind of husband whose wife decided everything for him, and, by the way, there are many husbands of this sort in Russia. But, later, after losing my temper somewhat, I stated that I would sign nothing voluntarily, and if they held me as they were threatening to do I would not talk to them at all.

At that the major put away the form and started filling out a formal warning about finding a job in the course of the coming month. It was expressed in rather vague language, speaking of responsibility but citing not a single article of the criminal code nor any decrees of the Supreme Soviet. Here again they had deceived me when they said at the outset that they wanted to speak with me without formal warning.

Two women were brought in, the witnesses, a middle-aged teacher and a young woman. The teacher kept exclaiming and sighing: How is it possible that you don't have a job! We bring our children up to respect work here! There was something touchingly provincial about her. These days one meets people of this type only in small towns.

I inquired whether they would give me a job in her school.

'We have only a few staff positions, a few teachers, and the supervisor of grounds and buildings.'

'That's it, supervisor,' I said. 'I'd make an excellent supervisor of grounds and buildings.'

In a reproachful tone, the major said, 'You should not make fun of people that way, Andrei Alexeievich.'

While this was going on the smiling duty officer had, on the major's instruction, already drawn up a report stating that I had refused to give them a written explanation. The witnesses both signed it, asking anxiously, 'We won't be put in jail, will we?'

I wanted to say that they would be locked up now if I did not find a job, but I recalled that one should not make fun of people.

We all were polite with one another. Neither the major nor the lieutenant bore me the slightest enmity: they did what they had been ordered to do, but without any enthusiasm. Only the prosecutor seemed angry, mostly because I had obliged him to work on a Saturday night.

Wishing to do something nice for the major, I said that I had told my wife about him and the apt remark he had made about the police.

He looked a bit uneasy, and the fellow in civilian clothes cocked an ear. Several months before, while I was petitioning for registration, I had been sent to Moscow and to Kaluga for permission. At the time I had said to this major, 'but this matter could have been settled on the spot; you're just making extra work for yourself.'

'It does not matter; there are a lot of us to make up for it,' said he, in the words of Zoya Kosmodemyanskaya.[12]

The fellow in civilian dress also exchanged a few words with me.

'You said you were a writer, didn't you? What do you write?'

'Plays.'

'*Will the Soviet Union Survive Until 1984*? Was it you who wrote that?'

'Yes, I. You mean you've heard of it?'

'I heard from Ginzburg when I was in Tarusa on business.'

Originally I had wanted to register at Tarusa and even had considered buying a house there, but was prevented from doing so because a KGB office had been opened there.

I remarked to this fellow that in Moscow it had not been the police but operatives of the KGB who picked me up. He hastily said, 'I have nothing at all to do with the KGB.'

They escorted me downstairs and returned my belongings. I hurried to a bus stop. It was seven o'clock in the evening. Within an hour I was at the railway station and around 10.00 p.m. was already coming into Moscow.

From the station I tried to telephone Gyuzel, but she was not home. Most likely, I thought, she was with the Rubins, with whom she had been waiting for me in the fifth precinct. So I decided to go to their place. On the way I planned to get off at Smolensk Square to buy a bottle of champagne in honour of my release.

The tube carriage was almost empty. Across from me sat a young man wearing a red scarf; on my left a little farther down there was another one.

How depressing it is, after all, I reflected, the way the system moulds people. Here are two of the first Soviet people I come across, and they have the faces of genuine stool-pigeons. With that thought I rose and went to the doors. The train was pulling into Smolensk Square. With a casual look, one of the young men got up, then, after him, the other.

It turned out that the store had already closed. Right around the corner stood one of my travelling companions from the tube. Without a backward look I went down into the tube, and, as luck would have it, the train was just pulling in. The passengers crowded in at the doors. I paused on the platform, the doors closed, and the train pulled out of the station. I stayed behind; so did the two young fellows in red scarves.

One of them approached me and said, with hatred in his eyes, 'How long, scum, are you going to play hide-and-seek with us?'

I had heard of instances like this before and was very nervous, as he continued, 'They let you go again, you bastard! They're going too easy on you! What's the matter, don't you understand? The party congress is just around the corner and we're not going to take any risks with our fine congress because of shit like you! Fuck off home and stay there! We won't lay a finger on you at home!'

I looked around – was there a policeman nearby, by any chance? Although recourse to the police at such moments does not help, nevertheless it is at least something to grasp at. I recalled the story of Pytor Grigorevich Grigorenko,[13] who, in the summer of 1968, was being shadowed by this kind of young man – true, only one – and Pytor Grigorevich went to a policeman and said, 'Some suspicious individual is following me, and I don't know what he's up to.' The policeman resolutely made for the spy and barked, 'Who are you? Why are you bothering this citizen?'

'I am not bothering him,' the spy said. 'I'm a locksmith.'

What policeman would stand on ceremony with a locksmith when Pytor Grigorevich Grigorenko still had about him the bearing of a general? So the policeman unceremoniously began to rub down the pockets of this 'locksmith', and from his breast pocket pulled a red KGB identification book. A mere glance at it, and he changed countenance and barked at Grigorenko, 'What do you want? No one is chasing you! Get on your way!'

On this occasion there was no policeman near at hand. The station was pretty well deserted.

'If one can speak quite frankly,' I said amiably, 'you have nothing to worry about. I am not planning to interfere with the party congress. I am not going home now; anyway, after those threats, I'd be afraid to stay home alone. So I'm going to some friends' place.'

'Go on to your friends, make it easy on yourself,' the police spy said, along with several obscenities. 'We won't touch you here, but on the street it will be just you and me. Then watch out!'

'The trouble is, as I see it, you're not the only one here,' I said. 'Yeah, there are many of our kind here,' he said, again in the words of Zoya Kosmodemyanskaya, and walked off.

I was not sure what the best move would be next. These might not be empty threats. Well known are the instances when KGB agents have beaten up people on the streets. For example, they fractured the head of Nikolai Zhuk, my friend from Magadan, and then for good measure put him into a psychiatric hospital for several months.

My house was right nearby on Vakhtangov Street, next to Smolensk Square, but I did not go home. Riding as far as Revolution Square, I left the tube, crossed Marx Prospect, and turned down Kuznetsky Bridge Street towards Telegraph Lane, where the Rubins lived, and where I now hoped to find Gyuzel.

As I walked along the now deserted Kuznetsky Bridge Street, I heard behind me the footsteps of the police spies, but I did not turn around. Back at Smolensk Square I had conceived a new plan. At the end of Kuznetsky, where it comes out of Lubyanka Square, I stopped by a glass door with a cream-coloured drawn curtain, and, although it was dark inside, I pushed the door open and went in.

The inner door proved to be closed. Through another entry into a small lobby there was a table and a box with a slit for papers. Just then, in the inner door with the same cream-coloured curtains, a small window opened and through it poked the face of a sergeant in a uniform with blue tabs.[14] This was a KGB reception office.

'What can I do for you?' he asked politely.

'My name is Amalrik. I would like to speak with one of your senior colleagues.'

He summoned the lieutenant on duty, who was quite young and apparently just out of officers' school. The lieutenant requested my passport, looked at it with surprise, and asked me to tell him what was the matter.

It was fairly useless to explain anything to him, but all the same I told him that the KGB agents who had been instructed to follow me were threatening to beat me up and all but kill me. The lieutenant left to call someone on the telephone. When he returned, he said, 'There are two possibilities: either you write out a statement now, or come back on Monday. The others will be here and can help you.'

'What good will that do, if they are going to smash in my head today?'

The lieutenant shrugged. 'What can I do?' Just the same I asked for some paper and wrote out a statement to the KGB telling how their people had abducted me and taken me off to Kaluga, and, on top of that, were now threatening me. As I was writing, a man in plain clothes entered from the street. He had a broad flabby face.

Taking no notice of me, he said to the lieutenant, 'How's it going, Vasya? Everything all right with you here?' He went inside, and the lieutenant reappeared at the window. 'That's our chief making his round of the posts. Do you want to have a word with him?'

I had already finished my statement and pushed it into the slot.

'Why not? I'll speak to him,' I replied.

In the corridor leading away from the rather spacious entrance lobby, the security chief met me smiling broadly from ear to ear. We entered a large office with a conference table. I briefly related to him the circumstances of my detention and the day's threats. 'Your colleagues are feeling jittery just before the party congress and acting a bit strangely with me.'

'There is something odd about what you are saying,' he said, his smile widening. 'The things you're talking about can get a person put in prison. Very likely they were not our people, but simply a bunch of hooligans of some sort.'

'Why would hooligans be concerned about the Twenty-fifth Party Congress?' I retorted. 'And, anyway, they knew exactly who I was. Look, I'm not demanding that you admit right here that they're your people, I'm not new to this game. If the authorities have instructed them to intimidate me, then my complaints are pointless. But if they are doing this on their own hook, that's a different matter. If they were ordered only to follow me and they are threatening to beat the hell out of me, then that's already disobeying an order, and it is imperative to punish any violation of orders severely. In old Mother Russia we can't get on without strictness. This is not some kind of America we've got here.'

Once again the chief smiled broadly and nodded. He liked the bit about strictness. I was reminded of an incident in the life of Voronel:[15] his police tails threatened him that if he were 'to run' they would 'rip his legs off', and the most they would get for it would be a reprimand. 'Is it possible to compare this? Here a person without legs and there only a reprimand?' Again the smile from ear to ear. He could make the comparison: a reprimand, or no legs. So?

'All right, all right. We'll report this immediately to our superiors.'

I asked them to give me their telephone number so that I could find out about my statement. The security chief, the duty officer, and the master sergeant all hemmed and hawed. 'You can find that in any reference book.'[16]

'All right, then give it to me from the reference book. I am not asking for Andropov's telephone number.'[17] (As it happened, my wife had already called Andropov that day, trying to find me.) They whispered a good while and gave me the number.

At a quarter to twelve I walked out on to the street. Kuznetsky Bridge was completely empty. I wondered: could my tails have figured that once I had gone into the KGB I would not come out again?

Only after I came out on Kirov Street did I notice one going along one side of the street and a second along the other side. I was afraid to go to Telegraph Lane by a dark side street, so I walked up to Kirov Gate, turned down Chistiye Prudy, and from there walked to Telegraph Lane.[18] Near Menshikov Tower I caught up with a middle-aged Jewish couple, the only people out on the street, and for a while I walked just ahead of them so they might be witnesses. I then rushed ahead and into the entrance of the Rubin's six-storey building. The elevator was not working. I climbed to the fifth floor on foot. No one had followed me inside, it seemed.

My heart was beating fast. I pressed the door-bell. No one came to the door. I pressed a few more times. From below I could hear careful footsteps: someone was coming up, then stopped half-way. I rang once more and slowly started down. I met a man in work gloves coming up. I could not make out his face, for, on seeing me, he turned back downstairs. When I passed the elevator in the main entrance, he was there intently tinkering away. It seemed to me just a trifle on the late side to be fixing an elevator at midnight on Saturday.

Outside there was not a soul walking. About ten yards away stood a car with a driver inside. I decided to go into the court-yard to see whether there was a light on in the windows upstairs. Possibly the Rubins were home and merely afraid to open the door so late. Scarcely had I turned into the entranceway when I saw that in the courtyard by the exit there stood three persons also looking up at the windows. It was too late to turn back, so I walked straight up to them. As I approached, I heard one of them saying in a loud whisper, 'Keep calm.'

Stopping a few paces away from them, but far enough in so that the fifth-floor windows were visible, I glanced up and saw that it was dark in the Rubins' apartment.

Not far away lived some other friends of mine, and I resolved to spend the night with them. Walking down Telegraph Lane I heard the car's engine start up. When I entered the completely deserted and dark Zhukovsky Street, an eerie uneasiness came over me. There was a slight frost, and the sidewalks and streets were icy. My heels struck the ice sharply, and just as sharply, I could hear the footsteps behind me. The street seemed endlessly long to me. The footsteps came ever closer, and I even heard someone panting just behind me. Either they wanted to frighten me, or they really planned to beat me up, or maybe they were simply afraid to lose sight of me; whichever it was, they were catching up.

I turned into the courtyard, and hurried up to the second floor. My friends certainly never expected to see me. Exactly twenty-four hours had elapsed since I had left the apartment of our friend the diplomat on Donskoy Street.

In the morning I went to the Rubins' place. It turned out that Gyuzel was not with them. She had returned home late the night before. The Rubins told how they had sat for a long while in the fifth precinct until Kiselev said to Gyuzel, 'What are you staying around here for? Your husband has been taken to the place of his residence registration.' They had not seen me taken away. The next day they had gone to Vorsino, the place of my registration. My landlord told them I had not turned up there. They then called Borovsk, and the policeman on duty told them I was not there. (Actually, I was brought in only two hours later.) They asked him to inquire in the district office of the KGB – 'The place is locked up,' he told them, just as in *The Life and Extraordinary Adventures of Private Ivan Chonkin*.[19] Back in Moscow, they had started calling the duty officer of the city police, who knew nothing. The telephoning was done by an energetic friend of Gyuzel's. When the duty officer hung up, she would call back again. Finally they phoned Andropov; by then I was already en route from Borovsk to Moscow. Andropov's secretary was pleasant enough and said: 'I sympathize with you but we have nothing to do with this matter. Put pressure on the police.' He acted as if he could not place my name.

The telephone at the Rubins' was disconnected. I called Gyuzel from a telephone booth and found she had left already. As we were getting a cab, not far off we saw a fellow hanging about whom the Rubins had noticed the night before and christened 'jug nose'. We had scarcely got into the cab when the driver, a young fellow but with the look of one who had been around, said in surprise, 'We are being followed.'

Behind us rode a car with the licence 'OBI'; neither from Moscow nor Kaluga, it was the very one in which I had been taken to Kaluga. For the duration of the party congress KGB 'workers' had apparently been brought in from various districts to cope with the crisis situation. KGB operatives of all varieties, accustomed to comfortable office jobs, were assigned to surveillance work on the streets, just as scholars are sent out to harvest potatoes. Later on, in the Arbat, an older man with a most imperious air strode and then ran in pursuit of us like a youngster.

I did not bother to memorize the licence numbers of the cars which followed us. They could be changed at will, and the next day the licence plate might be taken off altogether. A friend told me that he once had been tailed by a car with different licence numbers front and back. While settling up with the taxi driver, I remarked, 'On top of this rouble, you are going to get some entertainment. Now they will interrogate you about what was said here.'

Since I could not be found anywhere on the preceding day, a rumour went around that I had disappeared without trace. I rang up correspondents from the Associated Press and Reuters, asked them to come around and told them everything that had happened to me.

Vitaly Rubin was not shadowed when he left my place, and

when Gyuzel arrived she said that no one had followed her either. But now she had only to go out to the store for a tail to materialize on the spot. Two automobiles were staked out near the house, one on the street and the other in the courtyard, with four or five men in each. Gyuzel witnessed a curious scene: a large automobile with foreign plates drove into our street, stopped right next to the car full of agents and switched on its headlights full. The agents' pale faces were illuminated and they fussed about in a panic. The foreign car instantly backed out, turned and drove off. Most likely somebody had simply driven in to turn around, but the effect was quite amusing.

The car stayed on duty all night. We consoled ourselves with the thought that although it was not very pleasant for us in the house under siege, for the people in the stuffy, smoke-filled car it must have been still worse. Gyuzel did see in the store, though, that one of them, while dogging her heels, managed to buy a bottle of vodka. In the hope that we might be left in peace, we decided to leave Moscow the following day, on the eve of the party congress.

Late at night Andrei Dimitrievich Sakharov[20] rang us on the telephone and asked whether I might come to see him the next day. I promised that I would, but as a matter of fact I was somewhat afraid that a trap might be set for me on the way to his place. It was not out of the question that all this surveillance had been set up because of the possibility of our taking some concerted action before the party congress. I now think, rather, that they were afraid of any steps I might take in connection with our intention to leave for the USA or Holland.

The next day Sakharov called back to suggest that perhaps it was not worth 'tempting fate'. Over the telephone he read an appeal for amnesty for political prisoners that he was proposing to make at the time of the opening of the party congress. In the middle of it, we were cut off. I called back – engaged. After a few minutes he managed to get through, and though his voice was barely audible, we finished the conversation satisfactorily.

Later in the day I called the KGB reception office; nobody answered. Then I rang up the head of the office, and once more repeated that their operatives were threatening me. He immediately asked, 'Who gave you my telephone number?'

All that day, 23 February, if we went anywhere by taxi there was a car right behind us; if we went on foot, the car stopped some distance away. No one approached us or said anything. The Arbat looked like a street in an occupied city: at every step there were police and military patrols and plainclothes characters, quite unambiguous as to line of work. The area was full of official vehicles. Gyuzel went into a sporting goods store to buy a knapsack. Instead of the usual saleswoman behind the counter there were unfamiliar people and another strange face at the cash register.

In the evening, laden with books and food – one even has to take along milk when going to the country – we set off for the Kiev station. On the train at the end of the car appeared the same cast of characters, but I did not look in their direction. At Vorsino, however, none of them got off the train.

To reach our village one must walk about one and a half kilometres partly by way of a dark wood. As luck would have it, many people got off the train and we walked in large groups. Several men, who stopped ahead of us, as if waiting for someone, put us on our guard, but it is possible that they had nothing to do with us. In Vorsino we had no sense of surveillance or being spied on, and I sat at home and calmly wrote these notes. Of course, I did not go to see the prosecutor, but sent him a telegram to say that if he had pressing business with me, he could drive up to see me himself.

Thus we walked those one and a half kilometres without incident, and around 11.00 p.m. we were tapping on the dark windows of the house in which I have a room. The next day, 24 February, in Moscow, saw the start of the Twenty-fifth Congress of the Communist Party of the Soviet Union.

What frightened me most about the episode was the nervousness of the authorities. At each new point in the affair it was as if they did not know what to do with me. The divisional inspector of the police had dropped by Vakhtangov Street on 18 February, excitedly asking where I might be. On the 19th they sent me an invitation from Borovsk for 26 February. Still earlier, by listening in on telephone conversations, they had found out that on the evening of the 20th I was to be out for dinner, and they grabbed me as I was leaving. For some reason they took me to the fifth precinct and spent a long time finding out what to do with me next. For some other reason they drove me to Kaluga and there again for a long time 'co-ordinated' among themselves. On the 21st they took me to Borovsk without returning my belongings as if they had intended to jail me there for ten to fifteen days – and unexpectedly released me after having given me only an absurd warning and an equally absurd invitation to see the prosecutor on the day of the opening of the congress. They advised me to travel to Moscow to consult with my wife, and then and there set up police surveillance accompanied by threats advising me to stay home at Vakhtangov Street whence earlier they had driven me out by all these same measures. And, finally, two cars and eight to ten men attached to me – no one I knew in Moscow was subjected to anything comparable during those days.

What was the purpose of it all? If they saw me as some kind of obstacle to the congress, would it not have been more simple to propose earlier that I leave Moscow? (V. Voinovich, after reading this manuscript, suggested rewriting this sentence as follows: 'If they saw me as some kind of obstacle to the congress, would it not have been more simple to cancel the congress?') Gyuzel and I ourselves had wanted to leave the day before the congress and had discussed it at home.

Generally speaking there is at first glance something odd in the actions of the KGB. Their entire treatment of me since my return from exile leaves the impression that they have been intentionally provoking me to actions regarded by them as hostile instead of giving me a chance to live quietly and not bother them. But even in their desire to remove me from Moscow, they acted strangely – they destroyed our country house in the Ryazan region so that only parts of the walls remain, as if a bomb had hit it.

Back in 1970 Boris Shragin[21] remarked that as the Soviet

civil-rights movement began to emerge from the underground and openly declare itself, so the KGB began to retreat into the underground and its methods started to assume an ever more criminal character, even from the standpoint of the state whose security it was called on to protect. In its actions, the KGB resembles not only an Arab terrorist group such as Black September, not only the Sicilian Mafia, but quite definitely some teenage gang; not only do they incarcerate healthy people in psychiatric clinics, not only do they kidnap them on the streets, severely beat them or threaten to beat them and poison them with drugs; they also destroy and burn down country cottages, steal money, slash the tyres of automobiles, spread slander by word of mouth and in print, send out anonymous letters in obscene language and use obscene language in like manner on the telephone.

For many years now I have been observing these people and have come to the conclusion that their dominant characteristic is a kind of childishness, or, more accurately, juvenility; they have the cruelty of teenage juveniles which comes from immaturity, the juvenile inability to understand anyone else's feelings, the juvenile inclination to deny everything that is 'not their own', the juvenile dominance of emotions over reason, the juvenile deceitfulness and cunning, and, most important, the juvenile vulnerability and touchiness. It is impossible to wound anyone so mortally by a word as a KGB agent and no one reacts so morbidly to any jibe as they do. That readiness to take offence, incidentally, that peculiar presumption of injury, is characteristic of policemen in countries where the police play an exclusive role. Amongst our own KGB personnel it really has developed to excess.

Anything to do with me they simply cannot take calmly. Apparently I wounded them deeply, somehow or other, the minute they laid eyes on me.

Yet perhaps there is in their actions both calculation and cunning, also rather childish at that. By exaggerating every incident of dissidence and even provoking people, the KGB is trying to show the party chiefs its importance and its indispensability to them. The KGB is of course indispensable to this system, but there are times when it inflicts more harm on it than good.

Ideologies in Soviet Society

As Amalrik explains in his own introduction to this essay, he develops here ideas originally advanced in Will the Soviet Union Survive Until 1984? *Written in February 1976, the essay was published in English translation immediately after Amalrik's arrival in the West in* Survey, No. 99, 1976. *The translator was Hilary Sternberg.*

'The wheel of ideologies' first appeared in my essay *Will the Soviet Union Survive Until 1984?* [which appeared in *Survey*, No. 73, 1969]. The thought [about the diagram] came to me at the last moment and that is why the diagram appeared there not on the pages where I am dealing with the problem of ideology. In 1974, when I was deported to Madagan, the local KGB officials gave me the published text of my essay and asked me to revise and renounce it. They even kindly provided me with the main lines of such renunciation in a written form. Although nothing came of this KGB-planned 'revision', the idea of looking again at my essay after five years has not been lost: already in Madagan I had begun to tackle anew my 'wheel'. A year later, after my return to Moscow, during the period when I had very little time, I returned nevertheless to my 'wheel', and wrote a new article on it. I thought immediately of publishing it again in your journal, sent it to you from Moscow, and when I arrived in July 1976 from Moscow to Amsterdam the printed galley-proofs of my article were already waiting for me there for correction. In this way the 'wheel of ideologies' turned from the village of Akulovo in Ryazan province to Madagan (in the Far East), and from there through Moscow and Amsterdam to you in London.

*

Let us define an ideology as a socially significant system of ideas held by one or another social group and serving to consolidate or change social relations. This may appear too banal a definition, but in any event, it will be as precise as is necessary for the purposes of this essay.

Although it is possible to speak of the de-ideologization of a part of society and even of de-ideologized societies, it is nevertheless hard to imagine a social group or even a single person totally lacking the rudiments of an ideology and totally unaffected by the 'politicization' of his environment and his awareness of his position in that environment. In an epoch of political crises there even appears a terrifying type of 'ideological man': as a rule, a person who is very energetic but lacks the ability that culture gives to make critical appraisals of his convictions, and the capacity for moral judgement that stems from belief in eternal values. When such a man becomes an adherent of an ideology, and that ideology becomes his substitute for culture and religion, it eventually reduces him to a ruthless automaton, while he reduces the ideology to a rigid set of dogmas.

Many Bolsheviks have provided the perfect example of such an 'ideological man'. The Bolshevik revolution with its subsequent 'proletarization' of society 'at the bottom' and 'bureaucratization' 'at the top' gradually produced a peculiar society with 'de-ideologized' masses and a compulsory ideology, acceptance of which is an admission ticket to the 'top'.* In the 1940s and 1950s a lively ideological movement began to make itself felt,

---

*The compulsion of a single ideology has not only made the masses indifferent to it but has also had a singular effect 'at the top'. The typical Party *apparatchik*, waging an entirely real struggle with other *apparatchiki* for promotion and power, but within the frame work of a 'single ideology', loses sight of ideology as a political doctrine expressing the interests of any militant social groups. To him, ideology is some sort of vague back-drop, while on stage the struggle goes on between specific individuals. This eventually forms in him a demonological vision of the world: in everything that happens, whether in his own or a foreign country, he sees not the operation of social forces, as in fact he ought to according to his professed Marxist philosophy, but intrigues by various crafty individuals. It was [the artist and sculptor] Ernst Neizvestny who drew my attention to this '*apparatchik*'s demonology'.

175

just at the junction of these two blocks, somewhere on the borderline between the de-ideologized masses and the ritual ideology of the élite, in the shape of underground Marxist groups aiming to re-invest Marxism in Russia with its old, revolutionary (instead of its present, conservative), character. Twenty years earlier it might have seemed impossible for any other ideologies to develop in the USSR.

However, this has not been the case. Over the last ten years, in Soviet society, at first in somewhat amorphous form, and later becoming increasingly well-defined, several ideologies have begun to take shape, either entirely unconnected with Marxism or extending its limits by a considerable distance. Clearly the appearance of these ideologies is a consequence of the development and growing complexity of Soviet society, in particular the relaxation of its ideological intolerance and the ever-increasing inability of its official ideology to react to changes in 'the country and the world'. The concrete forms that these new ideologies (new, that is, for our society) have begun to take were influenced, as far as we can judge, both by Russian pre-Bolshevik traditions and by Western example.

Since only one ideology continues to be officially permitted and only one party is allowed to represent it, the other ideologies have failed to gain more than a very small number of open supporters, let alone come to their logical conclusion, the founding of political parties.

However, this makes it all the more interesting to begin studying them while they are still, so to speak, at the foetal stage. Ideological struggle in the fullest sense of the word, the struggle of ideas, the struggle of minds and for minds always precedes actual political struggle, sometimes by a considerable length of time. Consequently, a close examination of embryonic ideologies, while not affording an opportunity for accurately predicting the future disposition of political forces, will at least enable us to define several alternatives.

Obligatory external uniformity gives a very misleading idea of the unapparent inside picture. In reality ideologies which, as I have already said, can count few overt adherents, may have many clandestine and also potential supporters, while among adherents of the ruling ideology there may be those who are not only indifferent but even hostile to it.

The position of official ideology, at first sight undisputed, is more problematical than might appear. Andrei Sakharov and Alexander Solzhenitsyn, for instance, disagree in their interpretation of its role. Solzhenitsyn believes that it is still of decisive importance in the determination of state policies; Sakharov asserts that it is merely a camouflage for the pragmatism of a de-ideologized élite. It seems to me, however, that it plays an intermediate role, and in addition is not, basically, a unified ideology. Although the observations on its role as a camouflage are correct and I have already referred to it earlier in this essay as a 'ritual' ideology, its force of inertia is nevertheless very great and it cannot be said that there are no people 'at the top' who still regard it as an ideology in the true sense of the word.

In 1969 I made a first attempt to examine the ideologies in Soviet society and – to my own surprise – found myself drawing an amusing diagram of ideologies merging into one another and forming a closed circuit, a sort of 'wheel of ideologies'. Unfortunately, I only made a rough sketch, and because I did not explain it clearly enough, not everyone understood it properly. I have now returned to it, revised and elaborated it, and I should like to submit it to the verdict of those who form these ideologies, as well as those who study them.* The present essay is simply a commentary to that diagram.

*In fact I would prefer to avoid the verdict of the latter, since they are the people who regard a criminal trial as the best way of evaluating any idea that does not appeal to them. In 1970 such a court examined and valued at three years' imprisonment my book *Will the USSR Survive Until 1984?* (Amsterdam, 1969), in which I wrote about, among other things, Soviet ideologies (pp. 8–10, diagram on p. 37). [Also in *Survey*, No. 73, Autumn 1969, p. 65, and see pp. 20–21 above.] When we examine the connections between ideologies, and their prospects, we must keep in mind the overall idea that the growth or decline in the influence of ideologies is linked with the waxing or waning in influence of the social groups on which the ideologies in question depend for their support. We must also grant, however, that in crisis situations a social group may relinquish – if only partially – its old ideology.

The structure of the scheme is as follows: taking three 'ideological levels', (1) super-ideologies or social philosophies, (2) ideologies proper or political doctrines, and (3) sub-ideologies or ideology-feelings, we represent them graphically in the form of circles within circles.

We shall term *liberalism* the social philosophy (super-ideology) within the framework of which the individual is inclined to identify above all with himself while acknowledging equally the rights of other, similarly autonomous individuals. We can assume that this philosophy attracts the most independent-minded and self-confident people: in social terms, people in the free professions and people with an interest in freedom of private initiative.

We shall term *Marxism* the social philosophy (super-ideology) in which the individual is inclined first and foremost to identify himself with the class to which he belongs, and to regard other classes as suitable for annihilation, subordination or assimilation. We can assume that this philosophy attracts, in the first instance, representatives of the 'oppressed' classes, needy, envious or embittered people, people who have 'nothing to lose', as well as intellectuals striving to destroy traditional culture from within. Should the representatives of this ideology seize power by violent means, it becomes the natural ideology of *apparatchiks* unsure of their power and of their own significance without power and hence embittered and aggressive.

Finally, we shall term *nationalism* the social philosophy (super-ideology) within which the individual is inclined above all to identify himself with his nation, regarding other nations as neutral, or hostile, alien formations. On the one hand this is the philosophy of traditional societies closely bound up with the land, and it thus attracts people with a romantic turn of mind. On the other hand, we can assume that it will also attract in the first instance representatives of 'oppressed' nations, nations suffering from the consciousness of their own inferiority in comparison with other, historically more fortunate, nations.

These super-ideologies are not separated from one another by impenetrable barriers, but are contiguous. They form the outer circumference of our diagram.

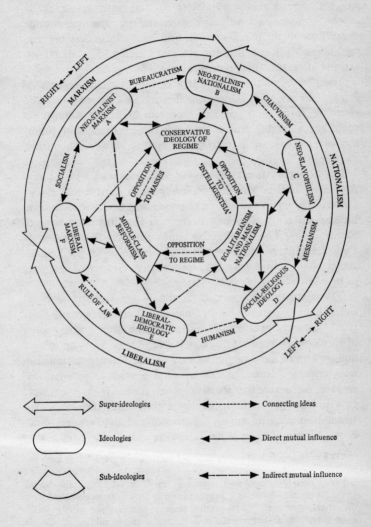

Super-ideologies

Ideologies

Sub-ideologies

Connecting ideas

Direct mutual influence

Indirect mutual influence

The middle ring consists of ideologies proper, not as universal in character as the super-ideologies, and with a specifically Soviet complexion. Although each differs, sometimes quite sharply, from the other, one can find connecting ideas between 'neighbouring' ideologies: the basic connecting ideas are shown on the diagram. The names of the ideologies are my own; representatives of them may disagree with my terminology. As I have already said, these ideologies have as yet no organized shape or form* and some of them are extremely diffuse; yet each has a 'right' and a 'left' wing, sometimes with intermediate gradations, its extremes linking it with 'neighbouring' ideologies.

Let us begin our examination of ideologies with *neo-Stalinist Marxism*. This is Marxism pulled through the needle's eye of Leninist theory of the seizure of power and Stalinist practice in holding on to it, then passed through the pragmatic sieve of Stalin's heirs. The social group which supports this ideology is that of the party and government *apparatchiks*, in the first instance of the centre. Its most representative figure would appear to be M. Suslov.[1]

The next ideology, going clockwise, is *neo-Stalinist nationalism*. This is a peculiar kind of national-Bolshevism, on the one hand 'under the banner of Marxism', on the other 'let the banner of Suvorov[2] be your shield', but Bolshevism brought up to date and pulling in the direction of ever greater Russian nationalism with antique Muscovite notions of a powerful, 'paternalistic' regime. Here too the social support comes from party and government *apparatchiks*, perhaps with a larger provincial representation. Linking it with the other official ideology, 'neo-Stalinist Marxism',† is the common idea of conservative

---

*The only legally existing party, the CPSU, is guided by at least two ideologies.

†Since both 'Marxism' and 'populism' talk of 'social justice' and 'socialism', it is possible for their followers to switch directly from one ideology to the other, or to converge for tactical reasons; but they are swiftly disillusioned, because at bottom the two ideologies are in mutual opposition, Historically speaking, Marxism emerged from liberal economic theories, while the populists in Russia were left-wing Slavophiles.

bureaucratism. It is customary to regard bureaucratism not as an idea but as a form of practice. However, what we have here is precisely bureaucratism elevated to the rank of an idea. In view of the Soviet leaders' striving towards depersonalization it is hard to say which of the representatives of 'neo-Stalinist nationalism' is the most conspicuous figure – V. Grishin,[3] perhaps.

The next ideology, this time unofficial, is *neo-Slavophilism*, which might also be termed 'romantic conservatism'. Its typical features are belief in the exclusivity of Russia and the need to revert to old Russian pre-Marxist and generally pre-Western traditions, and great interest in Orthodoxy. It contains the rudiments of a 'complete world philosophy' and will scarcely be tolerant of other ideologies. Although it is hostile to the official ideologies, its right wing is linked with 'neo-Stalinist nationalism' by the idea of chauvinism. However, the humanist features characteristic of 'neo-Slavophilism', which is a kind of 'nationalism with a human face', are utterly alien to 'neo-Stalinist nationalism'. As a nationalistic ideology, 'neo-Slavophilism' can count on very broad-based support, from the urban and rural semi-intelligentsia as well as from the more general public. Since the concepts of 'nation' and 'tradition' are very closely linked with language, many writers are the finest exponents of this ideology, the most typical among them being, perhaps, Alexander Solzhenitsyn.

We come next to '*social-ethical ideology*', which from the traditional point of view one could also refer to as a 'populist' ideology. It is an ideology which attempts to formulate ideas of social justice based not on economic determinism but on certain moral postulates. Its connection with 'neo-Slavophilism' is the common idea of Russian messianism: belief in Russia's special role and a belief that Russia has given, or will give, the world perfect and unique forms of human society. This too is a traditional Russian ideology and is capable of attracting sizeable sections of the intelligentsia who are disillusioned with Marxism but have populist inclinations. Evidently also it answers certain deeply felt popular needs. Very typical of its right wing was the All-Russian Social-Christian Union for the Liberation of the

People[4] headed by Igor Ogurtsov; however, for its left wing, for the moment at least, what is characteristic is simply an ethical attitude.

The idea of humanism, the acknowledgement of the value of the individual human being, links the left wing of this ideology with *liberal-democratic ideology*. 'Liberal–democratic ideology', which grew under the influence of Western liberalism, believes in the desirability of gradually transforming the Soviet system into a Western-style democratic, pluralistic society which would take account of the structure of property-ownership that has developed, but in which society would have effective control over the economy and there would be considerable freedom for private initiative. The social group supporting this ideology would be a considerable part of the 'middle class', a concept which overlaps but does not totally coincide with that of the 'intelligentsia', the word more usually employed in the Russian context – all those people who are not only active and educated enough not to lose their bearings in a free society, but will even achieve a certain success. We can regard Andrei Sakharov as a spokesman for the left wing of this ideology and Yury Orlov as representing its right wing.

The next ideology, *liberal Marxism*, is connected with 'liberal–democratic ideology' by the common idea of the rule of law, that is the establishment and strict observance of laws guaranteeing, in particular, human rights. 'Liberal Marxism' is the ideology of 'socialism with a human face' applied to the Soviet Union. It envisages the democratization and pluralization of society, while retaining Marxism as the leading ideology and the Communist Party as the leading political force. The social support for this ideology comes from a sizeable part of the middle class raised on Marxism and including, as far as we can judge from fragmentary data, many Party functionaries and industrial managers. However, this is, so to speak, the invisible part of the iceberg. The most distinguished spokesman for the right wing of this ideology is Pyotr Grigorenko, and for the left, [historian] Roy Medvedev.*

*I use the expressions 'left' and 'right' in this essay only as conventions

'Liberal Marxism' is connected with 'neo-Stalinist Marxism' by the common idea of building socialism. This connection is rather like a tiny, narrow tube between two communicating vessels, which might allow the adherent of each ideology to flow into the other under the impact of events.

Thus the 'wheel of ideologies' is come full circle. Let us now pass on to the sub-ideologies or ideology-feelings, which form the inner circle in our scheme.

We begin with the *conservative ideology of the regime* since this is in practice the ruling ideology. It is the instinct for self-preservation expressed in more or less ideological terms. Like any feeling associated with an inferiority complex, however, it is extremely aggressive. It is the emotional sustenance of, and is ideologically sustained by, in the first instance, 'neo-Stalinist Marxism' and 'neo-Stalinist nationalism', but is indirectly connected with 'liberal Marxism 'and 'neo-Slavophilism' as possible lines of retreat.

Egalitarianism and mass nationalism is even more of a feeling than an ideology, and does not figure in any dissertations or directives, although it is possible to trace popular moods. This ideology-feeling may be termed 'passive–explosive', since it is apt to break out abruptly, through its passive acceptance of reality and its desire simply to 'live', into sudden, usually individual outbursts. Should these become group outbursts, they will represent a great threat to the stability of the Soviet system. 'Egalitarianism and mass nationalism' are directly connected with 'neo-Slavophilism' and 'social–religious ideology', and at the same time are indirectly influenced by 'neo-Stalinist nationalism', which is linked with the popular idea of a powerful regime, and by 'liberal–democratic ideology', which answers the people's

---

within the clockwise directional system I have chosen for the graphic representation of my thesis. In this sense one can say that for three quarters of a century Marxism in Russia has travelled leftwards, from the liberal Marxist Struve to the nationalist Grishin, but has ended up on the right, going from left-wing liberalism to right-wing nationalism.

craving for a higher standard of living after the Western example.

Finally, there is *middle-class reformism*, the generally conformist approach to reality that is typical of the middle class, the attitude expressed as 'in the meanwhile we have to live, and gradually things will improve more or less of their own accord'. It is combined with the desire to avoid any sharp upheavals and sudden changes in any direction. 'Middle-class reformism' has a direct ideological connection with 'liberal–democratic ideology' and 'liberal Marxism', and also an indirect link with 'neo-Stalinist Marxism', in so far as part of the middle class consists of Party and government functionaries, and with 'social–religious ideology', in so far as it is a national ideology that to a certain extent answers the moral requirements of the middle class.

To conclude this description of our scheme of ideologies, something should be said about the peculiar negative links between the sub-ideologies. The 'conservative ideology of the regime' and 'egalitarianism and mass nationalism' are drawn together by their common opposition to 'the intelligentsia' as a stratum hostile to the people and dangerous to the regime, a connection emotionally reinforced by the fact that many Party and government *apparatchiks* were once peasants and the children of peasants. 'Egalitarianism and mass nationalism' and 'middle-class reformism' are drawn together by their common opposition to the regime, from which both these social groups are 'alienated'. 'Middle-class reformism' and 'the conservative ideology of the regime' are, in their turn, drawn together by their common opposition to the masses, in whom both the *apparatchiks* and the middle class see a threat to their privileges.

While I submit these three 'ideological circles within circles' for serious consideration, I should stress yet again the theoretical nature of the scheme, the blurred form of the ideologies I have singled out and the vagueness of the social stratification of Soviet society, as well as its low level of 'ideologization' in spite of the fact that the word 'ideology' is referred to at every turn – a kind of dialectical unity of opposites. If we take youth, as is often done, as an indicator of public attitudes, we see that it is, on the whole, totally indifferent to ideology as such. At the same time, this de-ideologization seems to me to be a temporary phenomenon, as it were, an 'ideological air-cushion' between moribund Bolshevik ideology and the ideology that will take its place. We cannot rule out the possibility that the youth of the 1980s will be highly 'ideologized'.

I should also like to make the reservation that the ideology represented by millions of *apparatchiks* invested with power, and the ideology represented by a handful of dissidents, play entirely different roles in society. Furthermore, an ideology in opposition and the same ideology in power are essentially two different ideologies.

The same can be said about an ideology in a pluralistic society and what may appear to be the same ideology in a totalitarian society: they are not identical.

Now, with the scheme of ideologies in front of us, let us play through a few versions of the Soviet 'ideological future'. For the sake of convenience we shall denote the ideologies, starting from 'neo-Stalinist Marxism' and going clockwise, by the letters A, B, C, D, E and F.

Let us separate the sheep from the goats, three of one and three of the other. We have every reason to assume that a stable society improves the chances of the 'middle ideologies' (A, C, E), i.e. those lying, as it were, at the midpoint of the super-ideologies, while a society in crisis improves the chances of the 'extreme ideologies' (B, D, F), i.e. those situated at the extremities where the super-ideologies meet. For example, we saw how, during the crisis in Czechoslovakia – a country with the same system as the USSR but with a democratic history – in 1967–8, ideological supremacy passed from 'neo-Stalinist Marxism' (a middle ideology) to 'liberal Marxism' (an extreme ideology). If the situation had stabilized there and Soviet troops had not intervened, I believe that the ruling ideology would have become 'liberal–democratic'. The stabilization achieved by Soviet intervention restored the supremacy of 'neo-Stalinist Marxism'.

Let us go further and divide the ideologies into pluralistic (D,

E, F) and totalitarian (A, B, C); alien–Western (A, F, E) and home-bred Eastern (B, C, D); ethico–political (C, D, E) and purely political (F, A, B). It is quite clear that in the USSR, in any imaginable political cataclysm, whether probable or impossible, the people who will have the greatest chance of survival and victory will be those who follow totalitarian and not pluralistic ideologies, home-bred Eastern and not alien–Western ideologies, purely political ideologies, not ethico-political ideologies burdened with all sorts of ethical notions of the kind the great Lenin so disliked.

It so happens that only one ideology meets all three conditions, and that is 'neo-Stalinist nationalism'. Since it is already one of the reigning ideologies and since, moreover, it meets the condition I earlier stipulated by being an 'extreme' ideology, in crisis conditions one may expect the regime to veer ever more strongly in this direction.

At the same time I believe that the chances of 'neo-Stalinist nationalism' are not all that high; its total victory might very well signal the beginning of a breakdown of the entire country. The fact of the matter is that, as a narrowly nationalistic doctrine, this ideology could only count on the support of the Russian population, who now account for no more than half of the total population of the country, while it would provoke hostility and intense annoyance on the part of all the other nationalities and their leading personnel.*

Let us imagine, however, that 'neo-Stalinist nationalism' wins. The most likely form for it to assume would be that of a military dictatorship. Yet to the extent that the situation stabilized, it might gradually become less rigid and begin to drift in the direction of 'neo-Slavophilism', a stable, 'middle' ideology.

However, since regional nationalism makes the chances of this happening extremely unlikely, perhaps we ought to examine another possible outcome of a critical situation: a swing towards 'liberal Marxism', an alternative extreme ideology.

A critical situation may be caused first of all by economic difficulties: a slowing in the growth of productivity, an inability of the agricultural sector to produce sufficient quantities of foodstuffs for the country, rising debts to the West and sinking gold and foreign currency reserves, the impossibility of reorganizing planning and economic management within the framework of a rigid political structure, and apathy on the part of the workers. It is not entirely impossible that, to the next generation leadership, perhaps more pragmatic and more tolerant, the ideas of 'liberal Marxism' may at any rate seem a lesser evil than a military–nationalist dictatorship. It is difficult to predict just how far such a process might go – indeed, if it were ever to begin at all – because this Moscow version of the 'Prague Spring' would suffer from a serious lack of historical liberal traditions of the kind that existed in Czechoslovakia. If, however, the process were to be crowned with success, as the situation stabilized the influence of the 'liberal–democratic', 'middle' ideology would grow stronger.

But these are all pure hypotheses.

*Central Asian nationalism may play a decisive role here in view of the high population growth of the central Asian republics.

A Russian's View of Freedom of Speech

This article was written on 5 August 1976, shortly after Amalrik left the Soviet Union. This translation was published in Crossbow, *Spring 1977.*

Such was the country and the time in which I was born and grew up that the very concept of freedom of speech long remained a mystery to me. When at the age of thirteen I composed a 'code of laws' for an imaginary country, I envisaged a three-year prison sentence for the expression of 'incorrect ideas'. When my aunt (whom I had acquainted with my legislative plans and whose husband had shortly before been sent to prison for 'slandering socialist reality') tried mildly to contradict me, saying that speaking one's mind was not yet a crime, a heated argument ensued. I tried to convince her – and she agreed – that if everyone suddenly started to say what they wished, total disorder and anarchy would, without a doubt, reign.

Unfortunately millions of my countrymen still think in this way. Not all of them consider the society in which they live ideal, or even normal, but, as for me twenty-five years ago, for them what is essential is uniformity of thought, or rather uniformity of correct thought. Some of them who have gone to prison in defence of their convictions still would not agree to their ideological opponents having freedom of speech.

One can arbitrarily break down freedom of speech into three stages.

Firstly, there is freedom of thought, when a person tries to give meaning to what is happening in the present, and tries to appraise it, consciously accepts or rejects appraisals made by others.

Secondly, freedom of thought demands freedom to say what

one wishes; the need to communicate one's thought to others and to obtain some sort of reaction must be satisfied, otherwise the unspoken thought will die, like an unborn child in the womb.

Finally, the need for communication between people is so great that freedom to say what one wishes – freedom of utterance – grows into freedom of the press when the utterance, through books, newspapers, radio and television, becomes available to practically anyone who wishes to acquaint himself with it. The right to read and listen freely is just as important as the right to speak and write.

Experience shows that these three stages are all parts of the same process. If freedom of the press is destroyed, then the freedom to say what one wishes, restricted to small groups, begins to wither and assumes a narrow, parochial character. If freedom of utterance disappears, then the idea in the head, trapped as if in a cell, inevitably begins to wither and die.

My country has passed through these three phases in the destruction of thought. After the complete destruction of freedom of the press, the exchange of ideas continued somehow in certain groups and families. But then fear and the activities of an enormous number of informers led those who still persisted in thinking to stop talking. However, it was impossible to think when one was deprived of the possibility of expressing oneself and of hearing others and was fed on a monotonous ideological diet. People stopped thinking or, rather, they came to think only within prescribed limits. If in the year that Stalin died complete freedom of speech had been proclaimed in Russia, it is highly unlikely that this 'great' country could have produced a single significant idea. Not only speech but ideas as well had been stifled.

Fortunately we are now witnessing the beginnings of the reverse process. One of the few Russian words which everyone understands without the need for translation is *samizdat*.

The realization of how necessary freedom of speech is for everyone was brought home to me when I realized how necessary it was for me myself, primarily as a writer. Words had become my profession and my *raison d'être*. But no sooner had I started to defend my right to freedom of speech when I received, one after another, three-year prison sentences. Those very same three-year sentences that I had, at the age of thirteen, prescribed for the promulgation of 'incorrect ideas'.

It would seem obvious that freedom of speech is necessary to writers, journalists – at any rate those who have anything to say – scientists and in general to those who are known in Russia as the intelligentsia. One might also claim that for those who are engaged in routine work unconnected with the use of words, who are obsessed with earning their daily bread, freedom of speech is a luxury, dispensable and not worth the risk.

Confirmation of this viewpoint can apparently be heard – in my country at any rate – on every side. Phrases like 'Live and keep quiet' or 'You've said too much' are a cynical indication that you have said something unwelcome to the authorities.

However my experience with people has convinced me that all this is quite untrue, and that the need to express oneself and to be heard is one of the deepest human needs. Unexpressed ideas, just like unvented curses, do not simply dissolve without a trace but destroy the human psyche and deform the consciousness.

A society which is deprived of speech is a mentally sick society. Just as a mentally sick person can appear normal, providing you don't ask him awkward questions, so a sick society can appear healthy to the untutored eye. But if you broach forbidden subjects – and there are quite a number in my country – then you'll get a pathological reaction. Western society relieves its tensions to a large extent by talking about its problems.

I'd like to end this article on freedom of speech with a cautious word of praise for censorship. A writer, and indeed the whole of society, needs obstacles to surmount in order to feel himself really free and to appreciate the value of freedom. A man who stands all his life in front of locked gates is in a tragic situation; the situation of a man who spends his life beating against gates which are already open may become comical. Thus the whole question of freedom is really a question about the limits of freedom.

The Speech of Andrei Amalrik Made on Receiving the International League for Human Rights 1976 Human Rights Award (9 December 1976)

The text of this speech appeared in English translation in the New York Times *of 3 February 1977 under the title 'By Bread Alone? A Well-Fed Slave'.*

Mr Chairman, Ladies and Gentlemen,

First of all, I thank the International League for the honour bestowed upon me as the recipient of the League's 1976 Human Rights Award. The occasion has extra importance for me because Andrei Dmitrievich Sakharov received this same award earlier, and the struggle for human rights in the USSR is linked, above all, with the name of Sakharov.

I believe that in awarding this prize to Sakharov and now to me you intended to recognize not us as individuals but rather the whole Human Rights Movement in the USSR – all those known and unknown men and women who proclaim to the world by word and by deed that freedom is not just an empty word.

In contrast to Andrei Sakharov, I can now speak directly to you. I feel that I am speaking not simply as the writer Andrei Amalrik; I am the ambassador of our movement, of those in prisons, in labour camps, in internal exile and in prison psychiatric hospitals who are defending their own dignity and thus everyone's human dignity.

I do not pretend that I have a mandate to speak in their name or that they would agree with all that I shall say here. But my participation in the Human Rights Movement, my experience of prisons, camps and exile, my striving always to write the truth, as well as the obligation imposed by your readiness to hear me out, give me the right and the duty to ask that you regard me as an ambassador of those whose voices can scarcely reach you through prison walls and the drumbeat of official propaganda.

When discussing human rights, we should keep in mind that there exist two categories of human rights: one category can loosely be termed civil rights, the second category socio-economic rights.

The first category includes the right of thought, expression, movement and association, in sum the right to display initiative – 'to do one's own thing'. This category of rights is most necessary to the more energetic members of a society. We can call the category as a whole the right to freedom.

The second category includes the right to gainful employment, to medical treatment, to social security, in sum the right to protection from social injustice. This category of rights is most needed by the less energetic but more numerous members of a society. We can call this category as a whole the right to security.

I have begun by distinguishing between these kinds of rights, but I wish to emphasize that human rights are in fact inseparable. And that increases the danger inherent in the increasing tendency not just to separate the categories of rights but to set one category against the other.

Some people say that in order to gain social and economic rights it is necessary to sacrifice civil rights. A less extreme view holds that it is first of all necessary to feed people and only then to worry about freedom of expression.

This view is, in the first place, immoral, and, in the second historically mistaken.

It is immoral because man has not only a stomach but also a head and a heart. To be fed is no great thing – a peasant feeds his horses so that they can work. A slave who has eaten his fill retains the psychology of a slave if he has never thought about freedom while he was hungry. If you respect hungry human beings, you should not only feed them but also convey to them a sense of their human dignity. Unless these two processes are to progress hand in hand, we shall live in a monstrous world.

Instead of giving $1,000 to each poor person as Senator McGovern proposed during his campaign, it is necessary to provide assurance that a person can earn money for himself, to provide education and work, and to make people aware of themselves as individuals.

The view which opposes one category of rights to the other is historically mistaken because wherever individual liberty has been sacrificed to achieve social and economic goals, social rights have suffered in comparison with their development in free countries. The USSR has more unemployment, lower pensions and worse medical services than the countries of the West.

The worldwide Marxist offensive is not, however, accidental. And it cannot be attributed solely to 'Kremlin plots' nor to such innate human emotions as hatred or envy, nor to the attraction of power which emanates from the USSR and which so impresses many people.

I believe that the success of Marxism can be explained by the fact that classic liberalism, the ideology which has shaped contemporary Western society, is experiencing a crisis, perhaps a fatal crisis.

I do not like the word 'ideology'. With the passing of the years I am increasingly convinced that the most important thing in life is human feeling, such as love for one's family and respect for one's friends. I recognize the evil to which ideologies have led. For some, ideology becomes a religion. For others, religion becomes an ideology. I do not know which is worse.

But I also recognize that ideologies are unavoidable – and needed, if they are viewed simply as tools to change the world.

The ideology of liberalism was one such tool, and it changed the world for the better. However, it failed to answer many questions. In effect, the liberal ideology throws a man into the sea and says: Sink or swim. The liberal credo is: Leave me alone and I will leave you alone.

It is this credo that is the apparent cause of the crisis of liberalism. People don't want to be left alone. They want others to care about them. They want something to be asked of them. They want something to be given to them. The knowledge that nothing in the world depends on you is a difficult burden to bear. Liberalism supplies no solution for loneliness or alienation.

And this is where Marxism enters the scene.

Marxism has placed its stake on force, which Marx called the midwife of history. And even though this midwife perpetually delivers monsters and not normal children, Marxists never tire of promising that the next child will be a splendid one.

I don't believe the Marxists. Many people don't believe them. But they have one great advantage. No matter how bad their prescriptions may be, they understand that the world is inexorably changing and they want to grasp hold of this change and direct it.

And what do the liberals want? What do they propose? To preserve what exists, to turn the clock back, to 'adjust to reality' – which means, in effect, making endless concessions to Communism in order to preserve a tranquil life for another year.

In this regard I am a leftist! I am one of those who understand that the world is changing and who want actively to shape that change. But I am not a Communist! I want to fight against Communism, but with my eyes directed forwards to the future, and not back to the past. I don't want to crawl backwards like a crab. I want to seek a new path.

I believe that everyone who values freedom is now facing the problem of creating a new ideology which will transcend both liberalism and Communism and make its central issue the indivisible rights of man.

Some people thirst for revolution. Others fear it. But which revolution is meant?

I want to contrast two revolutions. The revolution which occurred in your country two centuries ago and the revolution which occurred in my country little more than half a century ago. During the past 200 years people from all corners of the world have flocked to your country. Almost as many have fled from my country during the past sixty years.

No better comparison of these revolutions is needed than comparison of their attitude towards people and people's attitude towards them. I am for revolution! But I am for a humanitarian revolution. I am for ideology. But I am for an ideology of humanism.

194

And now, in appealing to you, I am appealing to the American revolutionary spirit. I appeal to your desire to sow the seeds of a new revolution, not to your desire to live undisturbed, paying for your tranquillity with credits, wheat and Pepsi-Cola. I appeal to the spirit of Jefferson and not to the spirit of Kissinger!

I am not afraid to utter naïve ideas. I am more of a realist than the exponents of so-called 'realpolitik'. You will never feel safe while you compromise with violence instead of fighting against it. The battle has been thrust upon you and you will not succeed in evading it.

I have spoken about going beyond Marxism and liberalism and creating a humanitarian ideology. I don't have a 'Humanitarian Manifesto' in my pocket. An ideology like this will have a long and difficult birth. And at the moment I don't know what mid-wife will bring it into the world.

In the creation of this new ideology, the unique and tragic experience which we Soviet dissenters can communicate to you should not be ignored.

The first Marxist revolution took place in our country, and it is in our country that the process of overcoming this ideology from within has first begun. It is a difficult, fumbling process, sometimes faltering, sometimes mistaken, but still I hope it will give birth to a new ideology. The Human Rights Movement in the USSR inspires this hope.

When we look at the Soviet Union, we are looking at an attempt to remake society, an attempt which has failed. Whether you wish to change the world or to prevent any change, you cannot ignore the lessons of this experience. And you cannot ignore those, however few in number, who have refused to accept its sham façade of success.

We are returning to the words 'freedom' and 'man', the meaning of which we – and perhaps you as well – had lost sight of. I ask you to remember those who are now incarcerated in prisons and labour camps and who are suffering in order that the idea of freedom should not perish.

I thank you again for the honour you have bestowed on me.

Eurocommunism before 1984?

Written in May 1977, this article was published in English translation in the International Herald Tribune *on 21 June 1977.*

The West is usually regarded as a society oriented towards change, a society in which the final say rests with children and not fathers, in contradiction to, say, many Eastern societies with their pursuance of permanence and their reverence for their elders. Not surprisingly, this orientation of the West favours those political forces which propose change – the forces of the left. Whether their proposals are good or bad is another matter.

The right, as a whole, offers only the preservation of what already exists, and instead of social and political changes has in mind only the maintenance or increase of economic growth. The politically thinking leader is being ousted more and more by the technocrat – a dangerous symptom demonstrating a lack of political prospects.

The left, whom the 'left–right' confrontation itself forces into a unity of a kind, is not in fact united. Left-wing democrats are sooner or later compelled to part company with left-wing totalitarians for whom the idea of equality is transformed into the idea of uniformity as a sort of surrogate for an equality that is unattainable in practice. However, this watershed of the left follows no clear-cut course; and it is precisely here that the game of Eurocommunism is unfolding.

It is a commonplace that the aspiration towards greater democracy and more independence from Soviet totalitarianism is both the essence of Eurocommunism, on the one hand, and, on the other, a tactical subterfuge. But where does essence end and subterfuge begin?

196

There exist, to my mind, two good criteria for measuring the sincerity of the Eurocommunists.

First, there is their attitude to opposition within their own party. If no opposition or free discussion within the party is allowed, it seems highly unlikely that, when the party comes to power, it will tolerate any opposition at all outside its ranks either. At a previous congress of the French Communist Party, Politburo member Roger Garaudy was unanimously expelled for revisionism; at the latest congress his programme was adopted just as unanimously but without any mention of his name. This is the kind of unanimity – unanimous rejection, and unanimous adoption of a programme – that is most frightening of all.

Second, there is the Eurocommunists' attitude to opposition, in countries where Communist Parties already hold power. The Italian Communist Party, albeit with extreme caution, talks of the need for the observance of human rights in the USSR. But its newspaper has not published a single letter from Soviet dissidents in ten years, although both Communists and non-Communists from the USSR have repeatedly appealed to it. When I sent a letter to *Unità* in response to an article which had appeared about me, the editor in chief of the paper replied that they only publish material expressing the viewpoint of the Italian Communist Party.

The coming to power of Eurocommunists in any Latin country will bring about changes in the party itself, and these will most likely not favour its 'Eurocommunist' elements. Let us picture the party's structure as a triangle whose apex and base (i.e., the leadership and rank and file, together with the electors who vote for the party) are composed for the most part of Eurocommunists with only a minority of Stalinists. The middle layer, however – the party apparatus and bureaucracy – consists largely of Stalinists who view any democracy as an obstacle to their work. It is these people, though, who will be the decisive force if the party comes to power.

It would not be stretching the point too far to call even the Bolsheviks after the February Revolution Eurocommunists. Until Lenin's arrival, Stalin occupied virtually the same position as Berlinguer today, and was proposing a sort of 'historical compromise': cooperation with the bourgeois provisional government. We know only too well, however, what Stalin developed into when he became the embodiment of the party bureaucracy.

For all that, I heartily agree with the Eurocommunists' argument that in their case it 'will not happen that way'. Indeed, what happened in Russia will never again happen anywhere. Marx long ago said that what first happens as tragedy later repeats itself as farce. But even the farce would be grim enough.

Evidently many people in the West indulge in the same degree of wishful thinking in their appraisal of Eurocommunism as they did twenty years ago in their judgement of Khrushchev's reformism. However, instead of the expected 'liberalization' of the Soviet system and 'convergence', what has happened in the USSR has been a gradual and disguised re-Stalinization.

The attitude of the right to the Eurocommunists shows that the former are totally lacking in any long-term political prospects. Fear of their 'own' Communists continually makes them try to please Moscow in the hope that, in exchange for their concessions, Moscow will play a restraining role. In reality, this has allowed the French Communist Party, for example, to create the impression of a party independent of Moscow, and at the next elections it will possibly bring that party into the government.

Those who encourage Soviet Communism are essentially powerless before the Communists in their own country. The right gambles on the ordinary man's fear of the Communists – but it is impossible to build one's entire policy solely on a feeling as negative as fear. In Italy, for example, it is evident that fear of chaos and disorder will soon prove stronger than fear of the Communists.

Let us suppose that the Communists come to power in Italy. We may safely assume that they will try to keep the managers in their jobs and will be careful with private property, but the first thing they will do will be to unify all the mass information media. Even now, many people in Italy are going over to the

Communists not because they believe in Communism but because they are certain the Communists will win.

A Communist victory in Italy may coincide with a post-Tito crisis in Yugoslavia and this will facilitate the bringing of Soviet troops into Yugoslavia. Not only Yugoslavia but Albania as well would then re-enter the Soviet orbit, with Greece isolated in the position of Finland, Italy in the situation of present-day Yugoslavia, and Spain in the position of present-day Italy. The southern flank of Nato would cease to exist, or rather, Germany and Belgium would be on the southern flank.

Of course, for this to happen the Soviet Union would have to surmount the internal crisis that is beginning to corrode its strength; but perhaps this is precisely how the crisis would be surmounted.

There exists a point of view according to which a Eurocommunist victory in Italy or France would be undesirable for the Soviet Union since it would create yet another independent form and centre of Communism in the world. If, moreover, this were a democratic Communism it would be too attractive to the Soviet peoples, while if it were totalitarian, its independence would represent a challenge to Moscow.

I cannot go along with this reasoning. An Italy Communist and freer than the USSR would in the final analysis have no more influence on Soviet citizens than Poland now has – which is also freer than the Soviet Union. A France Communist and totalitarian might be no more independent than totalitarian Romania.

A French or an Italian Communist regime would feel too unsure of itself both at home and in relation to its Western neighbours to carry through policies that were independent of Moscow. On the contrary: the USSR would be their only guarantee of holding on to power, and this would force them to accept any and all Soviet conditions. Even a colossus such as China was for a long time unable to afford the luxury of a rupture with the USSR.

Of course, it is not inevitable that the Eurocommunists will come to power; meanwhile, they may even play a positive role in opposition. The very phenomenon of Eurocommunism may yet undergo lengthy evolution, and here two dialogues seem to me of importance.

First, the dialogue of the Eurocommunists with the powerful – the US leaders, who can give them some room for manoeuvre, some opportunity for breaking away from the USSR without fearing the USA. Second, their dialogue with the weak – the dissidents from the USSR and Eastern Europe who can remind the Eurocommunists where Communism leads when it is built by violent means. The Eurocommunists' rejection of such a dialogue, or their readiness to enter into one, is in itself a good index of how democratic they are.

Although at the present time Eurocommunism is meeting with resistance chiefly on the part of the right, I believe it can only really be overcome from the left. A new ideology that succeeded in striking a balance between freedom and security and made its basis the inviolability of human rights would mean the end of the ideology of Communism.

The Movement for Human Rights in the USSR

Written in March 1977, this history of the twelve-year-old human rights movement in Russia appeared in the Paris Russian-language paper Russkaya Mysl (La Pensée russe) *on 30 June and 7 July 1977 and, in condensed form, in the Washington* Post *on 5 June 1977 and in the* Journal of Current Social Issues, *Summer 1978. A French translation was published in* Libération *on 27, 28 and 29 June 1977.*

Almost twelve years have elapsed since the birth of what was known at first as the Democratic Movement and – more recently – as the Movement for Human Rights in the USSR.

In the broad sense of the term, the Democratic Movement comprises all those, irrespective of their methods and ultimate goals, who struggle for the democratization of the Soviet regime, for the enhancement of the rights of society and restriction of the power of the state (all the while bearing in mind that the Western concept of 'society' is inapplicable to the USSR, where the powers of the state are virtually unlimited). In a narrower sense, the Movement embraces all those who consider themselves its members.

I shall use the term 'Democratic Movement' in the first as well as the second sense – not always, unfortunately, clearly distinguishing one from the other.

The beginning of the Movement

Khrushchev's reforms, notwithstanding all their contradictions, were a response to society's general aspiration towards liberalization. For this reason the attempts of the post-Khrushchev

201

leadership to reverse the process could not fail to arouse opposition, especially since, during the Khrushchev thaw, society had unfrozen and already begun to feel bolder than before.

The first confrontation between the authorities and society came with the arrest of the writers Andrei Siniavsky and Yuli Daniel.[1] On 5 December 1965 a small protest demonstration, organized by mathematician Alexander Yesenin-Volpin and the late poet Yuri Galanskov, took place in Moscow. This demonstration, demanding an open, public trial for the two writers, may be regarded as the beginning of the Democratic Movement.

The trial was not open, but staged by the authorities as a show trial: the newspapers vilified the two defendants who had published their works abroad and meetings were held condemning them. However, the result was in fact the opposite of what the authorities had intended: the trial proved that human dignity can be preserved even in the dock, and that it was possible to have a political trial in the USSR without the defendants 'repenting', a trial at which they in fact won a clear moral victory over their judges.

If anything, the trial roused the public to fight, and the form of struggle was one familiar to many societies living under dictatorship – modest petitions addressed to the authorities appealing for open trials, for more lenient sentences, for an end to repressions and no return to Stalinism.

The official response was to stage yet another instructive show trial, this one involving the young writers Alexander Ginzburg and Yuri Galanskov, the first of whom had published a 'White Book' on the Siniavsky–Daniel trial, the other the literary–political *samizdat* journal *Phoenix*. Yet, once again, their arrest in January 1967 and trial a year later were catalysts to public opinion instead of stifling it.

Shortly after the arrest of Ginzburg and Galanskov, biologist and writer Vladimir Bukovsky, then aged twenty-four, organized a protest demonstration in their defence and was himself arrested, but at his trial he upheld the human right to freedom of expression. Pavel Litvinov[2] was called in by the KGB and warned that if he prepared a collection of material on the

Bukovsky trial, he would himself be arrested. Litvinov then did something unprecedented: he had transcribed his talk with the KGB and now he made it public.

Neither Galanskov nor Ginzburg would admit their guilt. Each day during the trial sympathizers of the two defendants, as well as numerous foreign correspondents, gathered outside the court building (for they were not allowed into the courtroom). It was thanks to their efforts that news of the proceedings found its way into the world press; with foreign radio stations broadcasting the news back to the Soviet Union, there was scarcely a single person in Russia who did not know about the protest movement. These examples were an inspiration and encouragement to greater activity, especially since the course of events in Czechoslovakia from the end of 1967 held out the hope to many in the USSR that a similar process of democratization was a possibility in their country, too.

The number of petitions and letters mounted from day to day. Moreover, no longer were they couched in timid language, no longer did they restrict themselves to individual miscarriages of justice, and no longer were they addressed exclusively to the Soviet authorities. Now the letters, whose signatories soon passed the 1,000 mark, were addressed to the Soviet public and the public of the world at large; their language grew increasingly bolder, and they dealt with Russia's path of development as a whole. Many of the signatories really expected that the authorities would take notice of them and revert to a policy of reforms.

It was at that time that the term 'Democratic Movement' first appeared. The KGB would later claim that, like every other evil idea, this term, too, was concocted in the West. In fact it was suggested in the spring of 1968 by Pavel Litvinov and myself. The Soviet regime had, to use the Marxist term, 'removed' the struggle between the concept of equality and the concept of freedom, since it represented a fusion of inequality and unfreedom. Thus the Democratic Movement drew into its ranks advocates of both freedom and equality.

The movement was not large, as indeed it could not be in a totalitarian country, but it united people from the most diverse social strata: writers, scholars and scientists dissatisfied with the absence of freedom of creativity; workers keenly aware of their inequitable status in society; Communists who realized the gap between theory and reality; people who had never believed in communism; former camp and prison inmates fearful of a revival of Stalinism; people who were mere children when Stalin died; those people who made careers for themselves within the system, and people whom that system rejected even before they had finished university. I have always been struck by the fact that people with such different experience and outlooks could find themselves on the same side of the fence.

It is impossible to say how many Soviet citizens regarded themselves as supporters of the Movement, since only a tiny minority actively showed themselves. I have no doubt that had it not been for the repressive measures taken by the authorities, a demonstration of, say, fifty people one day could well have attracted 50,000 the next. It is easier to do an approximate analysis of the composition of the Democratic Movement, based on what is known about the 700 or so signatures to the letters protesting against the Ginzburg–Galanskov trial. Eighty-eight per cent of the signatories were members of the intelligentsia, 5 per cent were students, and the remaining 7 per cent workers. An analysis of 200 participants in the Movement arrested in 1969–70 shows the following percentages: intellectuals – 62, students – 14, workers – 34. The difference is explained, for one thing, by the fact that the authorities dealt more harshly with students and workers than with intellectuals, and for another, because a good many students and workers were arrested not for having written protest letters but for belonging to underground organizations.

Questions of programme and organization arose as early as 1968, until which time the Movement had been more of a shapeless, spontaneous phenomenon. Generally speaking, the participants fell into two groups, the 'politicals' and the 'moralists'. The former saw the Movement as an embryo of a political party, and wanted to work out a programme of political and socio-economic transformations of the Soviet system; the latter, either as individuals or collectively, simply wanted to assert the principle of morally repudiating and opposing the evil committed by the Soviet regime.

A compromise, probably unconsciously so, between these two positions was the 'legalist' movement, which demanded, first, that the Soviet government observe its own laws and, second, that it bring them into conformity with international law. As early as the 5 December 1965 demonstration in Moscow the slogan 'Observe Your Own Constitution!' was put forward, and a good example of the continuing insistence on this principle is the journal *Chronicle of Human Rights in the USSR*, which has been appearing in New York since 1973 under the editorship of Valery Chalidze.

But, however important the legalist movement was in a country that knew no legality, it lacked any 'charisma', and was unable to offer the majority of people a genuine alternative to the accomplished system represented by official Soviet ideology. On the other hand, Soviet society at that time was patently unprepared for the creation of new political programmes or parties. Thus, for instance, the anonymous 'Programme of the Democratic Movement of the USSR', which appeared in *samizdat* in 1969 and was intended as a kind of party programme document, met with scarcely any response. Furthermore, the Programme focused all its attention on the question of what our society ought to be like, and completely passed over the issue of the methods of bringing this about.

Now, however, I believe the problem is one of elaborating a completely new ideology as the basis for offering society a specific ideological programme, an ideology that would prevail over the largely discredited Marxism, as well as of authoritarian nationalism and classical liberalism. Yet all this is easier said than done!

The problem of organization, of creating a working group – necessary whatever the Movement's orientation – had also arisen in 1968, but had come up against a powerful psychological barrier. It seemed that if a human rights committee were to be openly established and formally constituted, all its members would immediately be arrested and sentenced to long terms of imprisonment; for this had happened with all secret organizations thus far, the moment the KGB discovered the groups' existence.

In 1969 this barrier was surmounted when the Initiative Group for the Defence of Human Rights in the USSR, comprised of fifteen people, came into being. Its members were not immediately arrested and it seemed at first as if the authorities intended to ignore its existence; but sooner or later ten of its members found themselves in camps or psychiatric hospitals on a variety of charges. Still, the foundations had been laid, and thenceforth various groups and committees were formed at intervals within the Movement and openly declared their existence.

Not only did the participants in the movements become actively involved in writing and distributing *samizdat* – on the initiative of [poetess] Natalia Gorbanevskyaya the newsletter, *Chronicle of Current Events*, was set up and has now been appearing regularly for nine years – thanks to the efforts of hundreds of people, a seemingly impossible phenomenon under conditions of Soviet totalitarianism.

The decision to send Soviet troops into Czechoslovakia was accompanied by massive repressions within the USSR. The 25 August 1968 demonstration on Red Square protesting against the invasion, however, demonstrated that the Movement had the strength to resist and oppose.

At the same time another important event took place: the publication of Academician Andrei Sakharov's essay 'Reflections on Progress, Peaceful Coexistence and Intellectual Freedom'. Sakharov's high position in Soviet society and his high principled morality not only assured him a leading role in the Movement, but lent the Movement itself a new lustre.

In retrospect, if I were to try to define the main characteristic of the Democratic Movement during its first years of existence, I would say that it was the priority it gave to speaking out against hypocrisy – the tradition of thinking one thing and saying or doing another. By openly stating their views, by raising the question of human rights and, simultaneously, of the individual's moral responsibility, the participants in the Movement began to loosen one of the invisible yet crucial pillars of the Soviet regime.

The Movement was anti-Marxist – not in the sense that it came out against Marxism as such – indeed, many of its participants regarded themselves as Marxists – but by virtue of recognizing that the transformation of human consciousness must take precedence over changes in the social and economic conditions of society. Now, ten years later, it is clear that the moral atmosphere in the country has changed – and is continuing to change. Which, of course, does not lessen the relevance of finding a political alternative to the Soviet regime; indeed, it makes the problem even more urgent than ever.

Crisis in the Movement

In 1969, partly as a result of government repressions, a period of confusion and decline began. The public, discouraged by the failure of the campaign of petitions and by the end of the 'Prague Spring', turned away from the Movement, which became more and more ingrown. The cycle of arrest–protest–new arrest–fainter protest became progressively more weakening: the Movement seemed to follow on the government's heels, its activity consisting solely of reaction to repressive acts.

Many people believed that the arrest and trial of Piotr Yakir and Victor Krasin[3] in 1972–3 together with the newly proclaimed Brezhnev–Nixon policy of détente signified the end of the Democratic Movement.

The 'repentance' and 'confessions' of Yakir and Krasin, two leading members of the Movement, brought in their wake a whole series of 'confessions' and had an extremely grave effect on both the dissidents themselves and on society as a whole, stripping the Movement of its moral charisma. This coincided with the departure from the USSR of both famous and unknown members of the Movement, who either preferred emigration to yet another arrest, or simply felt that the struggle was useless.

In addition, the new-born policy of détente transformed the Movement from an ally of the Western democracies (which was how it viewed itself) to an irritating obstacle blocking the path to Western–Soviet *rapprochement*. The problem of human rights was a nuisance to both right-and left-wing politicians in the West, who would have liked to reduce it at best to a matter of giving humanitarian assistance to particular victims of repression or people wishing to emigrate. While the Democratic Movement regarded openness and publicity as one of the most important means of changing the Soviet system for the better, the Western supporters of détente in effect wanted precisely to do away with that openness, declaring that all humanitarian questions should be examined and discussed with the Soviet authorities behind closed doors. The effect of this attitude was to encourage the spread of Soviet 'doublethink' in other parts of the world: one could think whatever one pleased about the Soviet system but say only what Moscow wanted to hear.

Internally the Movement was criticized from two opposing sides – the Christian democrats felt that the Movement's programme was no more than a continuation of Khrushchev's reforms, and that it was even the work of the Party itself; while the liberal Marxists, as a whole, charged the Movement with lacking a coherent programme, with using romantic methods and outright provocation. They asserted, for instance, that collective appeals to the government merely handed the KGB ready-made lists of potential victims.

Both these points of view contained some truth, but were in essence neither accurate nor fair. Both lost sight of the fact that the fundamental aim of the Democratic Movement was the restoration of human dignity in our country, without which any socio-economic or even religious reforms would be worthless. No more accurate was their low estimation of the value of appeals to the authorities: they ignored the vital importance of engaging the government in a dialogue. In retrospect, their appraisal of the worth of the Movement itself has proved incorrect: the Movement has not perished; time has seen it grow ever stronger.

The crisis of 1970–73 had yet another interesting result: while the Democratic Movement itself barely kept going during this period, it had already by then given a powerful impetus to the democratic movements of various Soviet national minorities, such as for instance the Crimean Tatars, already agitating for a return to their homeland, and the Jewish movement, campaigning for the right of emigration to Israel. The Crimean Tatar movement had come into being before the Democratic Movement, but Tatar participation in the Democratic Movement, as well as the participation in the Tatar movement of such famous democrats as Piotr Grigorenko, publicized and brought their campaign into the spotlight of publicity, in the final analysis forcing the authorities, little by little, to grant concessions. The Democratic Movement had a similar influence in the Ukraine, Lithuania, Georgia and Armenia.

The Jewish movement to emigrate to Israel had also arisen before the Democratic Movement. However, until the Democratic Movement – and Jewish participation in it – provided a powerful stimulus, it had been virtually unknown and almost entirely ineffective. The same was subsequently true of the Volga Germans. The Jewish movement, enthusiastically supported from abroad, for a time overshadowed the Democratic Movement: the Western press, for instance, treated the issue of the right of free emigration from the Soviet Union as a simple question of Jewish emigration.

One may say that all the nationality movements in the Soviet Union, both those which seek the right of individual emigration and those which seek to secede as nation states or to secure their national rights within the Soviet Union, may each be divided into two groups of supporters: those who feel that the nationality movements should not concern themselves with 'other causes' and those who feel that their own, national problems can only be resolved by way of participation in the Democratic Movement as a whole entity.

Since the end of 1973 the Democratic Movement has become increasingly more active and wide-ranging; it now calls itself the Movement for Human Rights (the struggle for human rights provides a broad enough basis to unite people with very different political points of view).

I feel that the publication of *Gulag Archipelago* (in late 1973) and the expulsion of Alexander Solzhenitsyn (in 1974) played a very important role at this time. The opposition-minded section of society was roused to action, and to halt the rising tide of protest the authorities again began arresting people, among them such famous participants in the Movement as Sergei Kovalev,[4] Andrei Tverdokhlebov,[5] Anatoly Marchenko[6] and Mustafa Dzhemilev.[7]

The award of the Nobel Peace Prize to Andrei Sakharov in October 1975 gave new impetus to the Movement for Human Rights in the USSR, showing as it did that the West's attitude towards this issue was gradually changing. This was of course heartening, and perhaps marked the beginning of dissident interest in the Helsinki Agreement, which until then had been generally considered a Western concession.

The setting up, in May 1976, of the [Moscow] Helsinki Monitoring Group, headed by Professor Yuri Orlov, was a new departure in the development of the Movement – and the authorities reacted very sensitively. The group is collecting and analysing all the material it can find on infringements of the humanitarian clauses of the Helsinki Agreements, and is making its reports available to the governments of the signatory nations. The group has also paid attention – for the first time in the Movement's history – to infringements of social and economic rights and, as a result, has come into contact with many workers, thus alarming and angering the authorities still more.

Crisis at the top

There are signs that the Soviet system is currently experiencing a power crisis – and the fate of the Human Rights Movement depends in large measure on how that crisis resolves itself. For a long time there existed a certain balance between the moderates and the neo-Stalinists at the top, a balance that ensured the stability of authority and the security of those in power. For the sake of maintaining that balance, the authorities had in the past tolerated the dissidents, applying limited but not massive repressions.

Now, however, all the high-ranking members of the Politburo are over seventy years old, and everyone is well aware that a change of leadership is inevitable simply as a biological matter of course. This is intensifying the struggle between the two power factions.

A similar situation had arisen in the late forties and early fifties, when Stalin's anticipated death prompted him, as well as extremists in the Politburo, to intensify repressive measures in order to preclude the possibility of any positive, liberal changes after his death. These tactics came up against the passive opposition of the more moderate elements in the Politburo.

This invisible struggle had highly visible symptoms which affected everybody: the so-called *Zhdanovshchina* (after Andrei A. Zhdanov, the Politburo member in charge of ideological affairs at that time), with its campaigns against 'bourgeois' intellectuals – writers and composers; party purges (the Leningrad and Mingrelian affairs); and finally the incitement of anti-semitism in the form of 'the struggle against rootless cosmopolitans'. Analogous, though far less extreme, situations can still be found today. The hysterical encouragement of anti-semitism by the country's leadership is in fact a characteristic of all Russian power crises throughout the twentieth century.

The struggle against 'cosmopolitans' culminated in January 1953 with the appearance of articles in the Soviet press about 'murderers in white coats' – Jewish doctors who had supposedly killed some Soviet people at the behest of 'International Zionism' and the American secret service. They were 'exposed' by a fellow doctor, L. Timoshehuk, who received the title 'doctor-patriot'. Several months later, came the death of Stalin and the arrested doctors were freed – and this signalled the victory of the moderates.

In March 1977 *Izvestia* published a letter by a new 'doctor-patriot', a surgeon named S. Lipavsky, a former member of the Jewish movement. In his letter Lipavsky said that this movement, like the Movement for Human Rights, was being directed by Zionist organizations abroad and by the CIA. Several days before the publication of this letter there had been a mysterious explosion in the Moscow subway – and semi-official statements circulated indicating that these explosions could have been the work of dissidents. Within a short space of time thirteen members of the (Moscow, Ukrainian and Georgian) Helsinki groups were arrested: Yuri Orlov, Alexander Ginzburg, Mikola Rudenko, Olesia Tikhii, Anatolii Shcharansky, Merab Kostava, Zviad Gamsakhurdia, Mikola Marinovich, Miroslav Matusevich, Viktoras Piatkus, Levko Lukianenko, Suren Masarian and Eduard Arutinnian.

In drawing these parallels I of course realize that the situation has changed greatly since Stalin's time: the structure of Soviet society has altered, the country is less isolated from the rest of the world than it was a quarter of a century ago, and there is an opposition which, though weak, makes its voice heard throughout the world. Lastly, of course, there is no Stalin.

Prospects for the Movement

There is real discontent in the country, and the Movement is its expression. In spite of repressions and the expulsion of some of its members from the USSR, it has survived for more than ten years, and, though it will experience crises, it will go on surviving. Its future, of course, depends on a multitude of political factors.

As I have already said, for the sake of maintaining political balance the Soviet authorities have avoided mass repressions, instead using a combination of arrest, compulsory hospitalization, job-dismissal and deportation abroad. Incidentally, the West doesn't quite seem to understand that emigration is not only, and not so much, a consequence of détente as a safety valve to let off steam, a gentle way of eliminating dissidents and potential dissidents.

Yet if the neo-Stalinists were to emerge victorious, and put an end to all openly voiced protest, social discontent may take the form of terrorist activity. The subway explosion was most likely the work of the KGB. But we already know of several instances of individual terrorism, bombings and arson that were not inspired by the authorities. If terrorist activities have not yet become commonplace, it is only because theory must always come before practice. The moment books and pamphlets ideologically justifying terrorism begin to appear, terrorism will spread throughout the country. The only reason such writings do not yet exist is because the Movement for Human Rights is the dominant force within the opposition. If this force were to be liquidated the inevitable result would be terror from below.

On the other hand, if the moderates gradually begin to dominate 'at the top', they will need the support of the Movement in order to cope with the neo-Stalinists. If the Movement approaches that moment without any sort of political programme, the chances of its exerting any influence will be slight indeed.

The greater part of the intelligentsia is dissatisfied with the existing state of affairs. But this is not to say it supports the Movement as a whole. The Movement disturbs people; it requires that they make choices – always an unpleasant dilemma for people whose capacity for action has been paralysed. Many are willing to believe the Movement is a dangerous provocation. Many who in their hearts are sympathizers feel that whatever they do, nothing can possibly be changed – an attitude even more paralysing to the will than fear. However, the intelligentsia as a whole is becoming increasingly disturbed by its false position in the Soviet system.

From the very outset, workers have always participated in the Movement, since, like anyone else, they set as much store by human dignity as by material well-being. However, they also demand answers to socio-economic questions. 'And what will you do with the factories?' is one of the first things any worker will ask a dissident.

The intelligentsia, most of which has only just 'come out from the people', does not want to 'go to the people', and so the gap between the two groups was until recently widening all the time. Now, however, the reverse tendency has appeared. Lately there have been attempts to find common ground with the workers – the events in Poland have set a good example to both intelligentsia and workers. Worker discontent is very strong, but they themselves cannot formulate it sufficiently clearly, or express it forcefully enough.

There exists a link which, though indirect, is clearly perceptible, the liberation movements of Eastern Europe and the Movement for Human Rights in the USSR. Favourable developments in Eastern Europe encourage the Movement, and vice versa. It is difficult to say, however, whether anything decisive can occur in Eastern Europe without preliminary changes in the USSR. As far as nationality movements in the USSR are concerned, the Movement will be able to play the role of conciliator in the future.

The Chinese threat is pushing the USSR towards the West, while criticism of Chinese totalitarianism indirectly helps to discredit the Soviet variety. In this respect the Sino-Soviet rift is a factor working for the Movement. The Chinese, incidentally, are following very closely all eruptions of dissidence within the USSR and the repressive measures taken by the authorities against them.

In the West, both left- and right-wing politicians, interested above all in preserving the status quo, take an unfavourable view of the Movement for Human Rights in the USSR, as a source of some anxiety. The entire economic policy of the West towards the USSR – including technological, financial and industrial input – is directed at stabilizing the existing, repressive Soviet regime. However, it is not out of the question that there are, or there will be, some politicians who realize that it is in the West's best interests to support the gradual democratization of the Soviet Union and the role of the Movement for Human Rights in that process. The very fact that there is openly expressed protest and criticism coming from within Soviet society cannot fail to exert an influence on various aspects of Western life. The development of Eurocommunism is one example of this.

President Carter evidently understands that politics, devoid of any moral foundation, gradually leads to the predominance of the desire for self-preservation above all else, and that the moral basis of Western politics may be precisely human rights (as distinct from national rights, as in the Third World, or class rights, as in Communist societies). The restoration to politics of a moral foundation of which unrealistic 'realpolitik' have deprived it, may enable the West to regain its lost self-confidence, and provide it with a new goal.

Furthermore, the United States has become convinced that once political coercion and hypocrisy are allowed to exist in one place, they begin to spread everywhere, including the West.

Therefore, if President Carter continues to adopt a hard line on the issue of human rights, the Soviet leadership will be forced to reckon with the Movement to a much greater extent. It is quite untrue to say that the latest arrests in the USSR were an answer to Mr Carter; they had been planned and set in motion earlier. As a matter of fact, I believe that Mr Carter's statement on that occasion saved many people from possible arrest, and actually led to the release of Mr Borisov[8] and Jewish doctor Mikhail Shtern.[9]

President Carter – a new man in international politics – succeeded in throwing the Soviet leadership into confusion; nobody had spoken to them in that way for a long time. There is of course the danger that, as Mr Carter gains political experience, he will move towards the more usual stance of Western politicians on this matter. The fact that the United States withdrew its inquiry about the Soviet Union in the UN Commission for Human Rights suggests that Mr Carter has in fact lost the first round of the fight.

But one can lose the round, and still win the fight.

1977
Utrecht–Washington

Editor's Notes

Preface
1. Dmitrii F. Ustinov, a former First Deputy Chairman of the USSR Council of Ministers, was appointed Minister of Defence with the rank of Marshal of the Soviet Union following the sudden death of Marshal Grechko on 26 April 1976.
2. This organization is usually known in translation as the Moscow Helsinki Monitoring Group. Professor Yuri Orlov was arrested in February 1977 and in May 1978 he was sentenced to seven years in prison camp and five years in exile for anti-Soviet propaganda.

Will the Soviet Union Survive Until 1984?
1. This exile is described in Amalrik's book, *Involuntary Journey to Siberia*, published in 1970 by Harcourt Brace Jovanovich in the United States and by Collins-Harvill in England.
2. The term generally used by historians to refer to the territory governed by the Kievan state, formed in the ninth century, as distinguished from the later Russia.
3. This took place in 1952 and appears to have been part of Stalin's preparations for a big new purge.
4. Another indication of a coming purge, this legal frame-up (with strong anti-Semitic elements) took place in early 1953, just before Stalin's death.
5. An opposition Marxist group at Moscow University.
6. Later published in the Russian-language journal *Grani*, No. 58, 1965, Frankfurt, Germany.
7. Published in English as *Into the Whirlwind*.
8. Published in English as *My Testimony*.
9. Some of these have appeared in English in M. Bourdeaux, *Patriarchs and Prophets: Persecution of the Russian Orthodox Church* (London: Macmillan). Many others have appeared in Russian-language journals outside the Soviet Union.

10. Poet and translator from the Polish, one of seven who demonstrated in Red Square against the invasion of Czechoslovakia, later arrested and confined to a psychiatric hospital; now lives in the West.

11. See Abram Tertz (Siniavsky's pseudonym), *Fantastic Stories* and *The Makepeace Experiment.*

12. See *This Is Moscow Speaking,* in Patricia Blake and Max Hayward (eds.), *Dissonant Voices in Soviet Literature.*

13. Their arrest took place in September 1965 and their trial in February 1966. Siniavsky was released in 1971 and left the USSR in 1973. He now teaches at the Sorbonne in Paris. Daniel, also released, is still in the Soviet Union.

14. Published in English as *The Chornovil Papers.*

15. Published in Russian in *Grani,* No. 52, 1962, Frankfurt, Germany.

16. Published in Russian by Possev-Verlag, Frankfurt, Germany. Most of the materials appear in Leopold Labedz and Max Hayward (eds.), *On Trial: The Case of Sinyavsky (Tertz) and Daniel (Arzhak),* (London: Collins-Harvill, 1967).

17. For materials by and about Kosterin, Grigorenko and Yakhimovich see Abraham Brumberg (ed.), *In Quest of Justice: Protest and Dissent in the Soviet Union Today.* Grigorenko and Yakhimovich were arrested in 1969 and confined to mental institutions.

18. See his book, *The Demonstration on Pushkin Square* (London: Collins-Harvill), also Brumberg, op. cit.

19. See his book, *Progress, Coexistence and Intellectual Freedom,* with an introduction by Harrison E. Salisbury.

20. See Brumberg, op. cit. Larisa Bogoraz-Daniel, the wife of Yuli Daniel, was exiled to Siberia, along with Litvinov, for participating in the Red Square demonstration against the invasion of Czechoslovakia.

21. K. van het Reve (ed.), *Letters and Telegrams to Pavel M. Litvinov,* Reidel, Holland.

22. See Brumberg, op. cit.

23. See Labedz and Hayward, op. cit.

24. See van het Reve, op. cit.

25. See Litvinov, op. cit.

26. Published in Britain by Longmans Green.

27. In May 1967 Alexander Solzhenitsyn addressed an open letter to the Fourth Congress of Soviet Writers demanding the abolition of censorship.

Editor's Notes

28. A reference to Stalin's purges of the entire Soviet hierarchy.
29. The 'economic reform' of 1965, involving some decentralization of decision-making.
30. This approach involves always putting the interests of 'the working class' – in reality, of the regime – above all others.
31. A reference to the slogan used by Czechoslovak reformist leaders in setting forth their aims.
32. Entropy: degeneration towards an ultimate state of inert uniformity.
33. This took place in June 1962. Several hundreds of the rioters were shot down. Novocherkassk is in southern Russia, near Rostov-on-Don.
34. The Great Russians constitute the bulk of the Slavic population of the Soviet Union. They are ethnically distinct from the other Slavs on Soviet territory, such as the Ukrainians and Belorussians.
35. A patriotic and chauvinistic Russian society formed at the beginning of this century. It organized pogroms against the Jews, often with official encouragement.
36. A club whose members glorify Russian culture and its history.
37. A film about the medieval Russian icon painter of this name, directed by Andrei Tarkovsky, who later made *Solaris*.
38. A phrase used often in the past to describe admiringly Lenin and the early Bolshevik leaders.

An Open Letter to Kuznetsov

1. KGB headquarters in Moscow.

I Want to be Understood Correctly

1. The Decree on Parasitism, under which judicial measures could be taken against unemployed persons.
2. Brodsky was, however, virtually forced into emigration in June 1972, and now lives in the United States.
3. A group of young Moscow poets who in 1965 popularized the practice of unofficial public poetry readings. The Russian initials SMOG stood for Boldness, Thought, Image, Depth, or, alternatively, the Youngest Society of Geniuses.

Are the USA and the USSR in the Same Boat?

1. The New Economic Policy, a partial return to private enterprise during the 1920.

One Year after Helsinki

1. Sergei Kovalev, a founder member of the Soviet group of Amnesty International, was tried in December 1975 and sentenced to seven years' imprisonment and three years' exile for anti-Soviet activities.
2. Konstantin Bogatyrev, a Moscow writer and scholar, was in April 1976 attacked and severely beaten up outside his home, and died of his injuries two months later.
3. In December 1976 Bukovsky was, however, 'exchanged' for the imprisoned Chilean Communist Party leader Luis Corbalan and flown out of the USSR. He now lives in London, where he continues to campaign on behalf of Soviet political prisoners.
4. See above note 2 to the Preface.
5. However, most other members of the group have since either been arrested or been made to emigrate.
6. Three of these writers, Erofeyev, Voinovich and Kornilov, are still in the Soviet Union, outcasts from the Soviet Writers' Union and hence unable to publish officially. The others are now all abroad.
7. In early 1975 Alexander Shelepin, Chief of the KGB from 1958 to 1962, paid an official visit to London at the invitation of the British TUC. The occasion caused considerable diplomatic embarrassment. In May of the same year Shelepin was ousted from the Politburo and lost his job as head of the Soviet Trades Union Organization, a post he had held since 1967.
8. Turchin left the USSR in October 1977 and now lives in the United States. An eminent physicist and computer scientist, he has taken up posts as a senior research associate at New York University and as a visiting scholar at Columbia University. His book *The Phenomenon of Science,* in which he discusses problems of evolution, intellectual development, scientific theories and totalitarianism, was published in 1977 by Columbia University Press.

Are There Political Prisoners in the USSR?

1. Kalmyk, Ingush and Chechen were three ethnic groups from the North Caucasus deported by Stalin on charges of collaboration with the Germans.
2. The Vlasovites were Russian troops led by General Andrei Vlasov against the Soviet Union after Vlasov's capture by the Germans in 1942. Vlasov was handed over by the Allies after the war and was executed.

3. The Bandera-ites were followers of Stepan Bandera, a Ukrainian nationalist who led anti-Soviet forces in the Ukraine after the Second World War until 1947 and who was assassinated in Munich by a Soviet agent.

Who are the KGB?

1. Ministry of State Security, their title from 1946 to 1953.
2. Felix Dzerzhinsky was the founder in December 1917 of the Cheka, the 'Extraordinary Commission', a force whose officially authorized aim was to 'hunt out and liquidate all counter-revolution and sabotage', and which later developed into the OGPU, a ruthless arm of the Stalinist terror.

An Involuntary Journey to Kaluga

1. *Evening Moscow.*
2. Alexei Amalrik, Andrei's father, was an invalid and needed his son's attention. He had suffered a heart attack and two strokes and had lost the use of his right arm and leg. He died in September 1965 during Andrei's exile.
3. The KGB headquarters in Moscow. Lefortovo is a KGB prison in Moscow.
4. See p. 135 above.
5. Published in 1970.
6. Vorsino is a small village south-west of Moscow. Borovsk is a district administrative centre, also south-west of Moscow.
7. A regional administrative centre about 150 miles south-west of Moscow.
8. The Ministry of Internal Affairs is in charge of all police in the Soviet Union with the exception of the security police (the KGB).
9. Kefir is a sort of yogurt.
10. All Soviet citizens must be registered with the police in the area in which they live and work. It is extremely difficult to move to major centres such as Moscow and virtually impossible for all former political prisoners.
11. When the sentence and exile terms have been served and the former prisoner has no further conviction on his record, the record of his conviction must be removed from his passport, but this is extremely unlikely in the case of political prisoners.
12. Kosmodemyanskaya was a high-school student and Komsomol member who volunteered to go behind the Nazi lines. She was captured after completing her mission, tortured and publicly

executed. Her last words are reputed to have been: 'There are many of us.'

13. A mathematician and cybernetics expert, a former general and a major leader among political dissidents, Grigorenko has been forcibly imprisoned in various psychiatric clinics since 1969. In the Spring of 1978 he received permission to visit the US for medical treatment and after two months he was deprived of his Soviet citizenship.

14. Light blue has traditionally been the colour of the secret police since before the revolution.

15. Voronel was a physicist and leader of dissident Jewish scientists. He emigrated to Israel on 28 December 1975.

16. Although Moscow has a population about the same size as New York's, it produces a telephone book only sporadically, and then seldom in printings of more than 150,000. When it appears it has the attraction of a best-seller and, when sold out, the value of a rare book.

17. Andropov is the chief of the KGB.

18. Amalrik is describing a small area almost at the very centre of Moscow and near the main post office.

19. A Soviet *Good Soldier Schweik*, a brilliantly humorous satire of the Soviet bureaucracy and military by Vladimir Voinovich unpublished in the USSR. Voinovich, a writer, playwright and film scriptwriter, was expelled from the Soviet Writers' Union in February 1974.

20. Sakharov is a noted Soviet nuclear physicist and champion of human rights. He was awarded the Nobel Peace Prize in 1975.

21. Shragin is a professor of education who emigrated to the United States in March 1974.

Ideologies in Soviet Society

1. Mikhail Suslov has been a Secretary of the Party Central Committee since 1947 and a member of the Politburo since 1955. In 1956 he was in charge of the suppression of the Hungarian uprising. At present he is Chairman of the Supreme Soviet's Commission on Foreign Affairs, and is regarded as second only to Brezhnev.

2. *Under the Banner of Marxism* was the name of a journal published in the 1930s in the Soviet Union. 'Let the banner of Suvorov be your shield,' was a remark made by Stalin in 1941 during the resistance against the German invasion. General Alex-

ander Vasilevich Suvorov (1729–1800) won fame in the Seven Years' War and later led campaigns in Italy and Switzerland against Napoleon.

3. Viktor Grishin is a member of the Politburo (since 1971) and of the Presidium of the Supreme Soviet; he is also First Secretary of the Moscow City Party Committee.

4. An underground organization formed in or about 1964, whose members were arrested and four of their leaders tried in 1967; some seventeen others were tried in 1968. Igor Ogurtsov, a translator from Japanese, now aged forty, was sentenced to fifteen years' imprisonment for 'treason' and 'anti-Soviet agitation and propaganda'.

The Movement for Human Rights in the USSR

1. Siniavsky and Daniel wrote under the unofficial pen-names of Abram Tertz and Nikolai Arzhak respectively.

2. Litvinov is a physicist, dissident and grandson of Maxim Litvinov, Minister of Foreign Affairs between 1931 and 1939 and then Soviet Ambassador to the USA between 1941 and 1943.

3. Yakir and Krasin were two prominent dissidents who, clearly under pressure, cooperated with the investigating authorities and were sentenced to three years' imprisonment and three in exile each, amidst carefully staged publicity for the benefit of the Western press.

4. See above, note 1 to 'One Year after Helsinki'.

5. Tverdokhlebov is a physicist and a former member of the unofficial Soviet Human Rights Committee founded by Sakharov in November 1970.

6. Marchenko is the author of *My Testimony*, a description of his experiences in Soviet labour camps and prisons from 1960 to 1966.

7. Dzhemilev is a Crimean Tatar leader and member of the Initiative Group for the Defence of Human Rights.

8. Vladimir Borisov was a former member of the Initiative Group for the Defence of Human Rights in the USSR who had been confined in various Leningrad psychiatric hospitals since 1969, when he was tried on a charge of having signed a letter to the United Nations and other documents.

9. Shtern was a Jewish doctor from the Ukraine who was arrested on trumped-up charges of accepting bribes from patients.

Acknowledgements

Preface to the Second English Edition © Andrei Amalrik, 1979, Translation © Hilary Sternberg, 1979.

An Open Letter to Kuznetsov © Andrei Amalrik, 1970. Translation © Peter Reddaway, 1970. *Survey*, No. 74/75, Spring/Summer 1970.

A Letter to Der Spiegel © Andrei Amalrik, 1970. Translation © Peter Reddaway, 1970. *Survey*, No. 74/75, Spring/Summer 1970.

An Author's Fight for Rights © Andrei Amalrik, 1969. *The Times*, 3 December 1969.

Foreign Correspondents in Moscow © Andrei Amalrik, 1971. *New York Times Review of Books*, 25 March 1971.

Amalrik on Trial in Sverdlovsk: Statement in Court and Final Plea © Andrei Amalrik, 1970. Translation © Amnesty International, 1970. *Chronicle of Current Events*, No. 17, November 1970.

Are the USA and the USSR in the Same Boat? © Andrei Amalrik, 1975. Translation © Hilary Sternberg, 1979.

One Year after Helsinki © Andrei Amalrik, 1976. *Observer*, 8 August 1976.

Europe and the Soviet Union © Andrei Amalrik, 1976. Translation © Hilary Sternberg, 1976. *Survey*, No. 100/101, Summer/Autumn 1976.

Détente and Democracy © Andrei Amalrik, 1977. Translation © Tobi Frankel, 1977. *Newsday*, 27 April 1977.

Are There Political Prisoners in the USSR? © Andrei Amalrik, 1978. Translation © Hilary Sternberg, 1979.

Who are the KGB? © Andrei Amalrik, 1976. *Far Eastern Economic Review*, 31 May 1976. Translated by David Bonavia.

An Involuntary Journey to Kaluga © Andrei Amalrik, 1976. Translation © Thompson Bradley, 1976. Reprinted by permission of the Alexander Herzen Foundation, Amsterdam.

DATE DUE

AP 27 '00